PRAYERS
FOR
IMPOSSIBLE SITUATIONS

LAURA GAGNON

Copyright © 2015 Laura Gagnon
All rights reserved.
ISBN: 10: 1519144806
ISBN: 13: 978-1519144805
CreateSpace Independent Publishing Platform
North Charleston, South Carolina

Table of Contents

Table of Contents

Introduction

The prayers in this book are crafted to touch the very deepest parts of the heart. Many people struggle with getting free and healed. Sometimes the struggle lingers for so long that it feels like we can be at a permanent impasse. The reality is, if we view any situation as one in which no progress is possible, we come into agreement with unbelief, and then we really do have an impossible situation. God doesn't move through unbelief. He responds to faith.

Prayer is simply conversation with God. It was never designed to be mindless or mechanical. God doesn't want our prayers to be drudgery. If you feel like you've been praying the same old stuff and your prayers don't seem to have the impact you'd like, then it's time to pray a bit differently. Difficult situations require different tactics. I pray you will allow this little book of mighty prayers to act as a guide to help you unlock the answers you need. Prayer should be *heartfelt* and *sincere*. Sometimes that's the missing element to breakthrough. I've come to realize that we can pray a multitude of prayers, but the ones that catch God's attention are the ones that are uttered from an honest, unpretentious heart. My desire is to help you receive a flood of answered prayer so that you, too, can proclaim, "Jesus really *is* Lord of all my impossibilities!"

The **difference** between the impossible

and the **POSSIBLE**

lies in a person's *determination.*

~ *Tommy Lasorta*

Chapter One

Do You Feel Trapped By Your Circumstances?

What do you do when you face an impossible situation? Whether it is financial, physical, emotional, or something else, everyone has situations that make them feel like they're boxed in on every side, lacking the necessary answers and change that they need. Physical, mental and spiritual exhaustion can begin to make one feel drained of vitality, faith and hope. What do you do when life becomes unbearable? What is the answer when hope is asphyxiated and people feel trapped by their circumstances? *Pray to the Lord of the Impossible.*

There are so many variables in each person's life and circumstances that it is difficult to address them all, but there are things one can examine to help diagnose a problematic situation. Sometimes people get so caught up in trying to deal with the difficulties of life that they forget to ask the important questions up front. Scripture gives us guidelines for many of the things we may encounter, but we cannot presume to know God's will about every situation unless we seek Him. When we find ourselves struggling with renegade thoughts, difficult circumstances or situations that seem determined not to give us a break, we must pray and ask the Lord, "What is Your will in this situation?" Perhaps a couple other very good questions are, "What do you want me to learn from this?" or "What action would you like me to take?" More often than not, when things aren't going well, figuring out whether we are trying to enforce our will or God's will can make all the difference. We need His perspective, His leadership, and His directives. Without them, we will end up struggling unnecessarily, lose our peace and joy, and feel completely frustrated. When we understand God's intention and we sense His leadership in our life, our spirit can find a place of rest.

In order for hope to find an anchor in our soul, it must be grounded in something steadfast, immovable and proven. Hope will turn to faith when it's anchored in something that has a proven track record of success. We have a rock in Jesus Christ; a solid, trustworthy person whose character is proven.

If a person is not a born again believer in Jesus Christ, they may well become a victim of circumstance. A person that confesses their faith in Jesus Christ, however, always has hope because God is bound by His covenant to honor His promises. When people look at their circumstances and feel that they are too overwhelming, they may feel it is impossible to change or break free from such limiting situations. It can be easy for a person in that state of mind to succumb to self-pity if they are not alert to that possibility. When life doesn't go as we hoped, it can be very easy to feel sorry for ourselves, but staying in that place too long can be dangerous. Complaining and bitterness provide an open door to the spirit of self-pity, and if the enemy finds it, the spirits of poverty, death and ruin come right along with it.

This might not be easy to read, but it does need to be addressed. Sometimes people enjoy the attention they get from their problems more than they actually want to receive a breakthrough. The sympathetic responses of others can feed a need to feel validated, recognized or affirmed. The person bound by self-pity and unbelief has actually traded in the truth in exchange for a false belief system built around the deception of the enemy. These things reinforce negative emotions that feed unbelief. We are all entitled to our emotions, but we must also guard our heart and mouth lest we drown ourselves in bitterness and misery. These things work together to cripple a person's faith. As unbelief grows stronger, life becomes a downward spiral that continues to paralyze the individual and make them completely trapped in their circumstances. The result is a person that has broken faith with God, and they may not even realize they have done so. The spiritual reality is that unbelief is aligned with rebellion towards God, and He cannot bless us when we are in agreement with the wrong things. He blesses faith and obedience. It is dangerous to adopt a victim mentality. Don't do it! The person that has their hope anchored in Christ, however, must make a choice to fight that lie and embrace the war cry of an over comer: *"I can do all things through Christ who gives me strength. Nothing is impossible with God!"*

- **Faith believes in God's ability.**
- **Faith declares the promises of God.**
- **Faith expects God to move on our behalf.**
- **Faith trusts the covenant relationship established by God.**

If you are feeling trapped by your circumstances, one of the first things to understand is the need to surrender every bit of it to the Lord. A need to control others or attempting to manipulate situations towards our desired outcome indicates the presence of fear and a lack of trust towards the Lord. If you have broken faith with God in some area or have spoken the wrong things, confess them so that they can be forgiven. God waits until we realize our own limitations and weaknesses and let Him have control. People often experience pain and frustration because they have not yet learned to let go and surrender control. There will be times when God wants to close doors or redirect us to something different. A person may never experience God's best if they insist on trying to stay where they are or keep doing what they've been doing - *even though their best efforts fail to produce a desirable outcome.* One definition of insanity is to continue doing the same thing over and over again, expecting different results. Friend, it's time to get off the merry-go-round! No matter what you're facing, you must be willing to trust God and surrender your storm!

Generational curses or spiritual blocks to prayer can be another reason why people often feel stuck in their circumstances. The spirit realm sees things much differently than we do. Demons know if they have a legitimate entry point into a person's life and thus are able to prevent answers to prayer from coming forth. Perhaps the best course of action is to ask God to show you if one of these issues could be a reason why answers to prayer are withheld. Blocked prayer is not necessarily the same thing as a generational curse, but both are important to address. This is not an exhaustive list of spiritual blocks to prayer, but some of them include: bitterness or unforgiveness, an attitude of unbelief or double-mindedness, slander or speaking against others in the body of Christ, personal sin, expecting God to move on our terms, misplaced faith, no personal relationship with God, asking for the wrong thing, murmuring and complaining, and idolatry. God has said in His word that His people are destroyed for lack of knowledge. The responsibility falls on us to determine where we might be missing an important truth. In one form or another, all sin comes from separation from our true identity, separation from others (broken relationships) and separation from God. These things can cause us to stay stuck in our circumstances until we address them properly – not according to our own feelings, opinions or beliefs - but according to God's word. Generational curses also keep people trapped in old cycles so that they cannot seem to move forward. When we are unsure of the reason *why* we are stuck or feeling trapped by our circumstances, if we will seek God for answers, He *will* send the answer we need. Perhaps the answers you've needed are within the pages of this book!

God is not daunted by the things that are beyond our control. He works outside the norm. It is not up to us to figure out HOW our prayers will be answered; simply to trust that He will. When life seems overwhelming and you feel frustrated, remind yourself that it's not your job to figure out the details. We have to trust Him to work in ways we do not always understand. God's ways are infinitely higher than our ways. He knows people we don't know, and He works with pieces of the puzzle we don't know even exist! As we trust Him to work out the details, He causes us to cross paths with those that He has chosen to bless us. His favor towards us is what compels others to release the things we need.

Part of getting 'unstuck' from your current circumstances is to have an understanding of your identity in Christ. Do you realize that there are some doors that will not open until you see yourself the way God wants you to see yourself? It is easy to feel defeated or unable to see a way out of your present situation if you don't know who you are or how to utilize what God has made available. A child of God has the same DNA as their Father. We are made in the image and likeness of God. Because the Spirit of God lives within us, the *power to create with Him resides within us.* Romans 4:17 reminds us that we have the ability to 'call those things that are not as though they were.' Truth displaces lies and has the power to restore faith. Faith comes by hearing the word of God. Faith assures us in our ability to use the authority God has given us. *The authority of God in the believer often times has the ability to create the breakthrough that is needed.* As we speak forth the promises of God, the way opens up before us. Sometimes we think we are waiting on God but perhaps He is waiting on us to get a revelation and run with it! Our pressing needs and a sense of desperation are not always what releases answers; *faith and obedience* moves God's hand.

Whatever your circumstance, God can make a way where there doesn't seem to be one. My husband and I have experienced many, many breakthroughs. It's when we thought we had nothing to work with that God moved. When we didn't have a job, God gave my husband a creative idea that led to work. When we didn't have any money in the bank, God had us start our own business. When one door closed, He opened another one. When we had no money to make a long but necessary trip to Canada, God provided supernaturally. When we moved on faith with no open doors where to live or work, God supernaturally provided. His favor does things for us that we cannot do for ourselves! When we didn't have a ministry, God launched one off of a little tuna casserole. When I miscarried and was told I wouldn't have any more children, my husband prophesied into an empty womb and it brought forth our son. We have so many testimonies of God breaking through difficult circumstances and those are just a few. Every one of them *seemed* impossible – until God showed up. When you place a demand on the anointing, faith pulls the answer out of the unseen realm. Your circumstances can change in a moment.

Never give up on the brink of a miracle! God delights in difficult situations because it creates a new story the world is waiting to hear. Your story could be next! All things become possible to him who believes. Would you like to encounter the Lord of all *your* impossible situations? "Call on the name of the Lord and He will show you great and mighty things you know not of!" Jer. 33:3.

Being challenged in life is inevitable.
BEING DEFEATED IS OPTIONAL.
~ Roger Crawford

Chapter Two

Believe

You may recall this story. In 2010 thirty-three Chilean miners became trapped when an underground mine collapsed. For the first 17 days the men were thought to be dead. They remained under the surface of the earth for a total of 69 days. The story captured global attention as the media followed the heroic rescue of the miners from 2,050 feet below the surface. They were between a rock and hard place, surrounded on all sides. They literally had to be *cut out of the rock*. Talk about being trapped by their circumstances!

It would have been easy for those men to lose hope, especially when the entire world believed they were already dead. Yet, God had a man hidden in the secret place that held on to his hope. The world had not yet heard of Mario Gomez, who had worked as a miner for 50 years. He went from obscurity to the limelight because his faith told a story the world needed to hear. Upon his rescue out of the escape capsule Mario said these words: "I never lost faith that they would find us." How could this man hold on to his faith when such grim circumstances surrounded him? Why did he not succumb to unbelief and hopelessness? Mr. Gomez, along with 32 other men, were trapped and hedged in by their circumstances in every sense of the word. By everyone's definition it was an impossible situation. The world thought they were dead for almost three weeks! Yet, all 33 men were safely rescued while the world watched a miracle in action. This man knew the secret to holding on until help arrived. Mr. Gomez' hope was not placed in man. His hope was anchored in God. This is just one amazing story, but it proves the loving care and commitment of our heavenly Father. His arm is not too short to save. He loves us so much that He will stoop down to rescue us and deliver us from our own impossibilities.

Impossible situations. We all have them. At some point we will face the temptation to throw in the towel, admit defeat and allow discouragement to claim our victory. If there is one thing I've learned along the way, it's the fact that God is the author of all our impossible situations, and He always has a plan to outwit the enemy. Don't give up!

One of the biggest things we have to confront in life is ourselves. It's not so much about the situation as what we *believe* about it. Every negative experience we encounter challenges our belief system. Negative experiences have a tendency to work against faith. Disappointment then attempts to rewrite the truth of scripture to fit our lack of understanding. This is because our heart demands answers to situations that cause us pain or discomfort. We may never have the answers for all of life's messes and disappointments, but a lack of answers does not mean that God's word is unreliable.

Our loving Father wants to give us peace, and one of the ways He does that is to elevate our perception and understanding of Him. Time spent in worship is especially effective at quieting our anxious thoughts and elevating our perception of God. When our faith is increased we understand that there is nothing that can stand against the authority of God! When we declare God's word and the name of Jesus over the situations that trouble us, sooner or later those things must succumb to the power of God's word. They have to, because spiritual laws are written into the code of every word in the scripture, and those spiritual laws govern the world in which we live. Even the most stubborn and resolute, difficult situation must bow the knee to the Lord Jesus Christ. Why? His name is above every other name.

His name is above sickness, disease and death.

His name is above poverty and lack.

His name is above loneliness.

His name is above grief.

His name is above injustice.

His name is above fear and everything you can name as a source of trouble that may come to your heart.

Philippians 2:8-10 declares: "Being found in appearance as a man, He humbled Himself by becoming obedient to the point of death, even death on a cross. For this reason also, God highly exalted Him, and bestowed on Him the name which is above every name, so that at the name of Jesus EVERY KNEE WILL BOW, of those who are in heaven and on earth and under the earth,..."

"The mountains melt like wax before the LORD, before the Lord of the whole earth." Psalm 97:5

Some years ago, the Lord awoke my husband and I in the middle of the night with the word, "Arise and thresh, O daughter of Zion!" Instantly I recognized the verse from Micah 4:13, which encourages us to beat down the things that rise against us. Even though we were tired, we got out the guitar and began to worship and make declarations. As we did, my husband heard the sound of demon bones being crushed under his feet. Now, demons don't have bones, but God gave him the understanding of what was going on spiritually.

Threshing is the act of conquering one's enemies. God gives His people strength to subdue their enemies. The word **'horn'** signifies strength and victory; and **'hoofs as brass'** indicates the act of having your enemies gathered under your feet, similar to oxen that tread on the grain to separate the chaff from the grain.

"Behold, I have made you a new, sharp threshing sledge with double edges; You will thresh the mountains and pulverize them, And will make the hills like chaff."
Isaiah 41:15

The mountains in our lives are the things that seem huge, insurmountable, stubborn or resistant. Sometimes those mountains are within us, and other times they come from external sources, like a health issue, a relational issue, financial difficulty or a spiritual attack. Whatever may currently seem like a mountain that is resisting the Lordship of God can be moved through the power of praise, worship and declaring God's supreme authority over that situation.

You will find that when you do these things, the *mountain* becomes a *fountain*. What was once a mountain becomes a fountain of living water. Who are you, O great mountain? Before the Lord Jesus Christ you will become small!

YOUR MOUNTAIN IS ABOUT TO BECOME A FOUNTAIN OF PRAISE!!
It's time for that mountain in your life to come down!
It's time for rivers of joy to flow into the dry places of your life!
Let every mountain become a fountain of everlasting joy as the God of Peace crushes the enemy under your feet!

Speak to the mountains in your life. Speak to the mountains of pride and stubbornness. Speak to that illness or financial crisis and command them to bow the knee to the name of Jesus. Speak to injustice, your fears, or whatever it is that you're dealing with. Declare the name of Jesus Christ over every situation that's been stealing your peace and joy. Tell those mountains Jesus Christ is SUPREME AUTHORITY and they must bow to the Lord!

One of the things people often struggle with is trying to determine if what they are praying for is God's will. The Lord is so good to us. Look in His word. Has He done it for someone else? 2 Corinthians 1:20 assures us that "*no matter how many promises God has made, they are YES in Christ. Through Him the AMEN is spoken to us by the glory of God.*" 'Amen' means, 'So be it.' Therefore, we bring our petitions to Him with confidence that we are starting off with a "Yes." God is Sovereign, of course. His determined will is ultimately the deciding factor in any given situation and it's our responsibility to accept that, whether or not we agree. We still pray to ask His will. His ways are not our ways, and we must learn to accept and yield to His Lordship. Hope can be found even in the situations that seem hopeless. Peace can be found in the midst of pain. The answers don't always come the way we anticipate, but His promise to us is that He will take what was meant to harm us and turn it around for good. Through prayer, we discover the weapons of the enemy are disarmed in the hands of the Lord. Therefore, we can rest in confident assurance that His desire is to answer our prayers. Answered prayer is what builds faith, and our Father desires our faith to be encouraged so that it continues to grow.

Beliefs are deeply ingrained in our psyche. When we have a belief that doesn't line up with the truth of God's word, for example, a struggle ensues that causes confusion, double-mindedness and a wavering between two opinions. Our mind is trying to determine what we really believe in order to settle the matter. We must learn how to settle our doubts. Doubt in any area will unravel faith and strip our prayers of the power needed to produce change.

The Amplified Bibles says it like this: *[For being as he is] a man of two minds (hesitating, dubious, irresolute), [he is] unstable and unreliable and uncertain about everything [he thinks, feels, decides]. (James 1:8)*

The CEB version says this: If you are that kind of person, you can't make up your mind, and you surely can't be trusted. So don't expect the Lord to give you anything at all.

And, the EXB version: Such doubters are thinking two different things at the same time [double-minded], and they cannot decide about anything they do [they are unstable in all they do]. They should not ·think [expect] they will receive anything from the Lord.

If we want to receive answers to prayer, we must resolve the double-mindedness issue, for God rewards faith and obedience. What we believe about God and what He has said in scripture ultimately determines our success in prayer.

The only way to settle the issue of doubt is to build up one's confidence in the word of God. Read it out loud! Faith comes by hearing the word of God. The word of God is anointed to produce faith when we speak it out of our mouth. We must make a decision whether we are going to believe God or trust in our own understanding and discard His words. Sometimes we need to repent for believing wrong ideas and placing our agreement with unbelief rather than faith. We don't mean to, of course, but that is why we need to know what the word of God has to say. Repentance involves changing our mind about something in our current belief system and making whatever changes are necessary so that we can draw closer to the Lord. These actions move His heart and His Spirit to bring a fresh wind of the Lord in our lives. It doesn't have to be complicated. It can be as simple as changing our mind about something that we once considered an acceptable belief or action. For instance, it is easy to form an opinion on a subject without all the facts; however when new information is introduced that we weren't previously aware of, it has the capacity to change a person's mind about something they once believed. Truth empowers us to make informed choices so that we reject wrong assumptions and erroneous beliefs. This change of heart is what leads us to change our old way of thinking. This allows us to come into agreement with God. All of a sudden, we agree with truth and we have positioned ourselves in proper alignment. God is able to then release the answer to prayer.

Whatever you believe for is what you make room to receive. It's a principle of agreement that actually produces an expectation in the spiritual realm. Faith is more than just something people practice in religious observance. Faith is a spiritual law. It is also a ***force***. Agreement is another spiritual law. We cannot expect to enforce the laws of the kingdom if we do not live by those laws. Unity of heart and mind among those that pray together produce powerful prayers. Even if it only between ourselves and God, we must have faith in order to be in agreement with Him. Jesus reiterated this kingdom principle of agreement in Mark 11:22-24. *"Have faith in God. Truly I say to you, that whoever says to this mountain, 'Be taken up and cast into the sea,' and does not doubt in his heart, but believes that what he says is going to happen, it will be granted him…"* We must come into agreement with God's word. Again, in Matthew 18:19 when Jesus said, *"Again I say to you that if two of you agree on earth concerning anything that they ask, it will be done for them by*

My Father in heaven. For where two or three are gathered together in My name, I am there in the midst of them." Unity produces alliances, interconnectedness and agreement that draw the presence of the Lord. The anointing flows freely where there is unity. His Spirit is intertwined among us as a three-fold cord that cannot easily be broken. When the conditions are met, He places His stamp of approval on our prayers and the answer is released.

Impossible is just a big word thrown around

by small men

who find it easier to live in the world they've been

given

than to **EXPLORE** *the* **POWER**

they have to change it.

Impossible is not a fact, it's an opinion.

Impossible is **not** a declaration, it's a dare.

Impossible is potential. Impossible is temporary.

IMPOSSIBLE IS NOTHING.

~ Muhammed Ali

Chapter Three
Courageous Determination

When truth comes up against a lie in your belief system, it causes a dying process to take place. That 'dying process' creates a war within the individual. The Spirit of Truth will always conflict with error and deception! That conflict can feel like anger, impatience, frustration, irritation, sadness and discouragement. If it feels like you're coming unglued it's because God is shaking your belief system. He allows us to feel unstable, confused, angry, hurt, and frustrated because this is how all the underlying, hidden falsehoods in our belief system make their way to the surface. This allows us to see where they enemy has been hiding. Time after time we read the words of scripture, *"Do not fear."* God reminds us to be fearless in facing the enemies of truth that try to hide themselves from us. We learn to focus on what God has said, rather than what our emotions are trying to convey. We put strength into action, apply wisdom and self control, and determine to utterly defeat the enemy every time he shows himself. We are *warriors*; we will not be defeated!

Joshua 10:5 tells a story about how Joshua found himself fighting against 5 ungodly kings that had assembled themselves against him at Gibeon.

..."Come up to me and help me, and let us attack Gibeon, for it has made peace with Joshua and with the sons of Israel." So the five

kings of the Amorites, the king of Jerusalem, the king of Hebron, the king of Jarmuth, the king of Lachish, and the king of Eglon, gathered together and went up, they with all their armies, and camped by Gibeon and fought against it. Then the men of Gibeon sent word to Joshua to the camp at Gilgal, saying, "Do not abandon your servants; come up to us quickly and save us and help us, for all the kings of the Amorites that live in the hill country have assembled against us."...

I want to give you a little insight into the meaning behind the names of these five cities.

- Jerusalem means **peace**. There is always a war for your peace!

- Hebron means **'to join, or team up.'** A company or a confederation of alliances. It can also mean to bind, and can be used in the sense of binding someone with a spell. Difference variations between the masculine and feminine part of the name indicated 'united, joined and bound together.'

- Jarmuth means **'to be high,'** either in literal height, or rank. It can be also construed as the height of pride or arrogance.

- Lachish means **'he who walks or exists of himself.'** This speaks of an independent spirit, or rebellion. It also means impregnable, fortified, obstinate, hard to capture, and invincible.

- Eglon means **'the bullock.'** A place of heifers, which speaks of strength. It also means **chief or king**, and round, or a circular round motion. Perhaps indicating a rolling about or going in circles.

Old Testament scriptures give us symbolic references to spiritual matters. Joshua's battle shows us a key as to how demons organize and strategize against us. He was in a battle against 5 very strong, stubborn spirits that were high ranking demons. They were full of pride, arrogance, and rebellion. These ungodly kings, (demonic strongmen), joined forces together and made them very difficult to defeat. They brought in a company of troops that arrogantly boasted they could not be captured, defeated, or evicted. This effect of binding themselves to people is what causes people to keep going around in circles. Demons manifest their character traits in those they oppress. They join forces in order to present a fortified wall of defense and attempt to resist being cast out of their host.

Joshua was a deliverer to God's people. When the Gibeonites called for Joshua to come help them, they were full of fear. The enemy had presented a very formidable picture of his alliances in order to intimidate the people into believing they were already defeated, but we can see from the biblical account of the story, this isn't true. Demons will always try to paint a false picture for people hoping they can convince them to give up before the battle is truly won. *The devil wants your submission.* It's all deception. The art of spiritual warfare is waged against the power of the lie. The truth is, a child of God has more power within them than the enemy does on his side, for it is written, ***"Greater is He that is in you than he that is in the world,"*** 1 John 4:4.

Delivering God's people is not always an easy job. People sometimes get so beat up from the enemy that they may want sympathy more than they actually want real change. Sometimes the words that God wants to deliver to people are not easy words to speak, and they're not easy for others to hear. There are times when a person needs the truth to really shake them up a bit. When people allow themselves to agree with the enemy and the results of their unbelief are destroying their life, what they need is a wakeup call. I've been in that place, too, and God never just allowed me to sit there and wallow in self pity! I would often get a stern rebuke, even when I most wanted sympathy! If that is how you sense your Father dealing with you, don't be offended. That's when you know He's talking to you like your Father. It's because He loves you and doesn't want you to become prey for the enemy to devour. He wants you to rise up and overcome. We must all confront our own faulty beliefs. If people don't learn to fight, it will be very difficult indeed for them to mature in Christ or develop any sense of stability in their faith. People must realize that they have been given an opportunity to raise their spiritual sword against the enemy and become the over comer in Christ that God says we are. Satan is relentless in his plan to kill, steal and destroy. We cannot afford to see ourselves from a perspective that places us in agreement with the enemy because that can align ourselves with rebellion.

Rebellion often looks very different than what we might imagine, and that's where we can fail to recognize our own blind spots. Whenever we are in agreement with attitudes or beliefs that cause us to feel unworthy, rejected, defeated, angry or accusing towards God, or feel that we can't trust God, we have rejected truth and accepted the lies Satan has told us. Thus, he becomes our god and master in those particular areas of our life because we've given away our dominion. Without even recognizing it, we can unknowingly enter into an ungodly peace treaty with the enemy and align ourselves with unbelief and the kingdom of darkness. This is why we can't trust our feelings to always tell us the truth.

- **Do not make a peace treaty with the enemy.**
- **Take the enemy by surprise.**
- **Pursue your enemy until you can put your foot on his neck and force his surrender.**
- **Forcefully advance the kingdom of God and slay the enemy. Leave no survivors that can regroup and attack again another day.**

While the Gibeonites were standing there shaking in their boots, Joshua got a word from the Lord to pursue the enemy (Joshua 10:8-10, KJV).

*And the Lord said unto Joshua, Fear them not: for I have delivered them into thine hand; there shall not a man of them stand before thee. Joshua therefore came unto them suddenly, and went up from Gilgal all night. And the Lord **discomfited** them before Israel, and slew them with a great slaughter at Gibeon, and chased them along the way that goeth up to Bethhoron, and smote them to Azekah, and unto Makkedah."*

The Hebrew word 'hamam,' used for **'discomfited'** in this portion of scripture means to make a lot of noise, confuse or route. Our English word for discomfit means unfasten, break up or disintegrate. By definition, the word means to cause uneasiness or embarrassment, to put someone off their game. It means to confuse, agitate, fluster, upset, disorient, disturb or unsettle. In other words, it means that if God is going to displace your enemy, He is going to have to rattle his cage a bit and put that devil on the spot. Holy Spirit will eventually pin him down so he has no more wiggle room to escape. This is why the use of scripture is powerful and effective. Scripture is anointed to route the enemy into a place of defeat. Once Satan's tactics are identified, the person can make a conscious choice to exercise their will over the enemy. The process can be uncomfortable, but, it becomes the moment of freedom for those that have been oppressed by the enemy. This is what it means to put your foot down on the enemy's neck just like Joshua did to those five ungodly kings.

We have to tell demonic spirits to unlink, or unfasten themselves from one another and come out from where they've been hiding. Then we command them to go back to the abyss and ask God's angels to lock them up until the day of their judgment. Joshua knew how to route the enemy to get them into a place where he could defeat them. He went to locate the five kings that were hiding out in a cave in Makkedah, trying to escape certain death. Their plan failed. Joshua brought out the ungodly kings and had them slain, and then he hung up their bodies as a warning to Israel's other enemies.

Every enemy must be destroyed if we are to have peace and good success. Demons will always try to hide from you, which is why God allows things to come shake you up a bit. He's trying to shake those demons out of the cave where they're hiding in your belief system.

Scripture defines Satan as liar and the father of all lies. He throws a fit when he's in pain, and truth causes him an incredible amount of anguish. If the Deceiver has been a false father to you, then let him die! The war within is to provoke the individual to make a decision what they really believe. Is your emotions truth, or is God's word truth? Is what you see in the natural the final outcome, or is there a higher plane of reality based on scripture, and what exists by faith? The person that makes their emotions the measuring rod to determine truth will always be unstable. This is caused by a spirit of double-mindedness and unbelief.

Feelings come and go. They are constantly in motion and are not a true barometer to establish truth. Scripture says the heart is deceitfully wicked, who can know it? Our hearts are fickle! One day it will tell you one thing and the next day it will tell you something else. Instead, recognize the plumb line established by God's word. The Spirit of Truth will make you free *when you choose to line up with truth.* The illusion is that the enemy is stronger than you are and you can't get free. This is not true. The spell of the enemy's deception can be broken once a person settles it in their heart what they believe and whom they will serve. You will be able to walk free because the truth has made you free; it's all a matter of choice. You really do have to decide who you are going to serve. The enemy will only listen to you when you exercise the spiritual authority God gave you, and that is through **declaring** the word of God. Every time Satan came to tempt Jesus, He responded with, *"Get away, Satan. It is written..."* and He would quote scripture. This is how you overcome.

When you break the agreements you've had with the wrong things, you can come back into right alignment with God. God will not put a blessing on disobedience, sin and our faulty beliefs no matter how much we pray, cry or beg. He teaches us to grow up in Christ by partnering with Him in our own self deliverance and we wage war using our spiritual sword and shield, (the Word of God). When God shakes you, He's trying to get *you* to shake off the old man. Shake off the old belief system! Shake off the father of lies! Shake off the agreements you've made unknowingly with deception and the enemy. Let the spirit of the Lord STAND UP on the inside of you and declare, *"Away with you, Satan. Get out!"* This is the day to say, "I'm not buying the lies anymore! Jesus Christ is Faithful and True. I break every agreement I've made with unbelief, double-mindedness, lying spirits, familiar spirits, rebellion, discouragement, depression and witchcraft spirits. I CHOOSE truth, and I choose to believe what God has said. This matter is finished, devil, now go to the abyss that was created for you and never return! In the name and authority of the Lord Jesus Christ I pray, amen."

However difficult life may seem,
there is always something you can do
and **SUCCEED** at it.

~ *Stephen Hawking*

Chapter Four

Persevere

Many Christians probably consider their hearts loyal to God. Peter thought he was faithful and loyal to Jesus, too. When he was tested, however, he discovered that his heart was not as loyal as he once thought. We really never know the depth of loyalty we have until we're tested in certain areas. Fear of persecution, loss and anger that result from deep disappointment challenges the loyalty of our heart. Pain is the real litmus test to examine the condition of our hearts. The enemy's goal is to unsettle the heart and attempt to damage the trust of our relationships. This is how he divides and destroys confidence towards the Lord.

I had many years of generational iniquity to overcome from my life. Familiar spirits and *familial* spirits (passed down from one family's generation to another) knew my weaknesses better than I did. They were so skilled in how they suggested lies...thoughts that sounded so natural to believe I accepted them as truth. The enemy's lies suggested God couldn't be fully trusted. Bitter memories enforced the idea that my heart was safer in my own keeping instead of entrusting it fully to Jesus. All these things worked against building a solid foundation of trust between the Lord and I. Bitterness prevented me from receiving the revelation of God's genuine love and character. One day God spoke: *"A root of bitterness has prevented you from seeing me as I really am. You have persecuted me, and believed me to be someone that I am not."*

That revelation floored me. It got my attention, and it began to set me free from a lifetime of deception.

You may have struggled and wrestled with God for what seems like your entire life. It's natural to want to give up when it seems that there are little results for your effort. There are some spirits that are more stubborn and resistant than others. Matthew 17:14-21 is a warning about stubborn spirits that don't give up easily. Jesus advised fasting along with prayer to help move the demonic spirit out of a boy when the disciples could not cast it out. When they brought the issue to Jesus, He told them that it was because of their unbelief. They were dealing with a stubborn spirit that did not want to let go of the child, and they became frustrated at their lack of understanding.

When a person has struggled for a long time with the same recurring issues they get weary, discouraged and unbelief sets in. The father of the boy in Matthew 17:14 struggled, too. He came to Jesus and pleaded with him to help his son. A demon had tormented this family for a long, long time and tried on multiple occasions to kill the boy. The disciples could not cast out the spirit. No doubt their faith was challenged when they heard the reports of how this demon harassed the child. The father was weary of dealing with it. He said to Jesus, *"If you can do anything, have pity on us and help us!"* Jesus responded by saying, *"**If** I can...? All things are possible to one who believes!"* Afterward, the disciples questioned Jesus why they could not deliver the boy. They were told it was because of their unbelief and that some demons only release their captives through prayer *and* fasting.

FASTING is a chain breaker. It helps break up the entangled root system so that it can be removed from a person's life. When you're dealing with a generational spirit, it's been there a long, long time. It's not going to give up easily. FASTING is a necessary component to help drive the enemy out! Couple it with worship, prayer, declarations of faith, and pronouncing God's word. If you remain persistent and determined, you can and will get free. It's hard, I know. We all want the quick fix, but everything in our journey becomes teaching curriculum in the hand of the Lord. He won't waste your experiences.

You might be wondering how you can tell for sure if you have a stubborn demonic root system at work in your life. Demons have a way of revealing our weaknesses and character flaws to ourselves. Let me give you an example. If you think of someone you're offended with and something rises up within you and says, "I am not going to forgive that person," you have a stubborn spirit working against you. If you begin to rationalize all the reasons why you're entitled to your feelings, there is a strong possibility that you are dealing with spirits of Defiance, Stubbornness and Rebellion. If you tend to justify all the reasons why you feel entitled to retain certain behaviors, activities or attitudes that are not in alignment with God's will, then you may be dealing with a stubborn demon. If you *feel* ornery and hard headed towards God, or you find that you consistently make allowances for your own behavior and excuses to resist repentance, that is a clue you have a very stubborn spirit at work in your life. It can come in through generational sin that runs in families, or it can be doors you've opened yourself, but the reality is some demons are stronger than others and thus become more difficult to remove from one's life.

Addictions, lust, rebellion, bitterness, anger, self pity and witchcraft (which is control and manipulation), are all very strong, defiant spirits that resist deliverance. Generational poverty is another one. When a person or a family has struggled under demonic oppression for what seems like their whole life, it affects their entire belief system. Poverty is a *mindset* of unbelief. When you are struggling with these sorts of spirits, it is difficult to believe God, much less trust Him. The demons are involved in an emotional tug-of-war; always trying to accuse God of being unfair, unloving, hard to please and other things that attempt to paint a wrong picture of Him. This is how the enemy keeps anger and distrust alive in the heart and mind of his victims. Satan the accuser always seeks an opportunity to divide and separate the person from the love of God. Fasting is a necessary component to soften the heart of the individual so that they willingly choose to yield to the will of God.

Have you ever tried to pull out a long rooted, stubborn weed out of dry ground? It's impossible. The root will break off and the plant just keeps growing back. If the ground is well saturated first, however, it is much easier to pull on that root and have it come up out of the ground. When the ground is saturated all the way down to the tip of the root, the ground around it gives way and the whole root will come out. This is a good example of how we pull out a spiritual root, too. Your heart needs to be well saturated in worship. Add the component of fasting along with worship and prayer, and then your heart will be pliable enough to yield to the will of God. Fasting humbles our flesh so that we can hear the Lord more clearly, and gain understanding of what we are to do. Ask Holy Spirit to show you exactly what you need to understand so that you can get free. This process breaks up the web of lies. When the Holy Spirit comes to tug on those stubborn roots, the resistance is gone so that they come up and out of the individual. The person receives their deliverance and healing becomes a life changing event. Persevere until you know without a shadow of a doubt *it is finished!*

Prayers

Prayer for a Right Spirit

Father God,

I thank You for loving me so much that you always offer encouragement. Create in me a clean heart. Let a right spirit be renewed in me this day. I give You permission to change my heart, my attitudes, or whatever needs to change so that I can receive life changing revelation. Forgive me for being stubborn or resistant. Let my soul breathe again, O God. If there is anything I need to see differently, please show me. If I have a wrong belief about something that is hindering me in some way, show me. Let me be awakened in my understanding. In Jesus name, amen.

Prayer to Heal the Wounded Heart

Heavenly Father,

I want to be free and healed. I do not want bitter memories to prevent me from walking into a blessed future. I surrender every lie, every bit of deception, every hurt and bad memory to You. I surrender the shame, rejection, self-hatred, self-pity, the feelings of condemnation, guilt and blame that I have turned inwardly onto myself, as well as those thoughts and feelings of judgment that I have placed upon others. I choose to forgive those that have hurt me (*insert names where possible*) and I ask that You forgive them, too. Heal their areas of brokenness. I receive by faith that You sent Your Son to die for my sins and that Jesus paid the price for my victory. I thank You that as I have chosen to forgive others, I can receive Your forgiveness for my sins.

Please unravel every lie that is based upon a false belief system, controlled by fear, insecurity or inferiority and held in place by the deception of the enemy. I willingly break every agreement I have had with the works of darkness. I let go of the past and all the disappointments that occurred. I release myself and others from judgments I've made. I choose this day to move towards healing. Therefore, I renounce all anger, unforgiveness, bitterness, jealousy, resentment and a desire for vengeance from those that I have blamed for my pain. I renounce the seed of every lie that I have taken into my heart and I ask, Father, that you would now cause those seeds planted by the enemy to shrivel and die immediately. Let them bear no more bad fruit. Holy Spirit, please visit me with your salvation and bring healing to my mind and emotions. Lead me into the truth that will unravel the lies and set me free. Fill me with the fullness of Your Spirit, which are wholeness, healing, life, light and purity. Fill me with a revelation of how greatly loved I am by God, and let that pure love wash away the pain and hurt. Please transform my thoughts and belief system to form new, healthy thoughts that are void of pain, mistrust, anger, unforgiveness, insecurity and inferiority. I pray that my responses demonstrate gratitude, self-control, love, peace and joy. Thank you for the victory and for realigning my future to walk into the newness of what You have for me this day. In Jesus' name, amen.

Prayer to Uproot Stubborn Spirits

Father,

I feel like I have struggled with the same issue for too long. I don't understand what is blocking my progress, but You do. Please help me get free and healed. Holy Spirit, I choose to yield to You. I ask You to reveal the thoughts, memories or insights that are needed so that my heart can release stubborn spirits. Show me the blind spots the enemy is working through. Lead me into worship. Lead me into the right frame of mind so that I am ready in every way to receive my healing. I give You permission to change my heart so that the enemy is defeated and I gain the victory. You may change my attitude towards whatever it is that is hindering me from getting free. Please give me the gift of Your grace, Your compassion and Your mercy that enables my heart to let go completely. I thank You for a new perspective that will release my healing. In Jesus name, amen.

Note: Incorporate fasting and saturate yourself in worship for the prayer to be most effective.

Prayer to Heal a Troubled Marriage

(Pray this with your spouse)

Dear Heavenly Father,

Help us shut the enemy out of our marriage and family. We repent for anger, power struggles, poor communication and dishonoring one another. We repent for any ways that we have rejected or disrespected one another. We chose to forgive each other of the past and we will not bring up old issues. We will not continue to blame each other for things that happened in the past. We repent for any sins of ourselves or others in our family line that led to adultery, jealousy, broken vows, and betrayal of trust or broken commitments. We ask that the sins of the past be broken off of us and forgiven. We ask You, Lord Jesus, to receive us as Your own. We believe You can heal our marriage and make it healthy. Let this be a brand new day.

We renounce fear, unloving spirits, anger, condemnation and criticism. We repent and renounce of any ways we have entertained fault finding. Today we ask for grace to modify our behavior, to know when to remain silent and appropriate ways of addressing issues. We ask for a release of Your love and grace to help bring lasting change. Give us eyes to see the positive things and help us bless those things deserving of praise. Help us to replace bad habits with good ones.

We come together now in a prayer of agreement, asking that you help us recover trust, love, honor and respect. Holy Spirit, forgive us for grieving you and not honoring Your authority over our marriage. We make a covenant with You now, and ask that You speak to us, bless us with wisdom and counsel from above. Help us to remember to honor You and ask You for help. Please protect our marriage from the plots and schemes of the evil one. Come and refresh our marriage. You can make all things new. You can resolve issues that on our own strength we cannot. Let the hurt feelings be washed away by the power of Your love. Breathe a fresh wind into us individually, but also into us as a couple. Fill us with Yourself, Holy Spirit. We need You. We cannot revive ourselves. Please, help us come back into divine order in all things and shut the enemy out of our thoughts, our responses, our family and our future. In Jesus name, amen .

Prayer for Wisdom
When You Don't Know What to Do

Father God,

Your word in James 1:5 tells me that when I lack wisdom, I can ask for it and You will give it to me. You know my situation with (_____). I do not know what to do. If I do nothing, nothing will change. Therefore, I must do something. I ask You for wisdom from Your Holy Spirit to know what steps to take.

I ask that You bring this situation to a point of decision. Show me clearly whether or not this situation is salvageable. If so, give me understanding of how it can be fixed. If other parties involved are unwilling to do what is necessary to correct, repair and mend this problem so that it can be healed, then show me that, too. Reveal the intent and motive of people's hearts so that I am not deceived. I ask that You would deliver me from confusion and put things in order. Lord, even if my heart gets broken, I need to know the truth. Give me grace and courage to carry out the changes that are necessary. If You know that I won't make the hard decisions that need to be done, then I give You permission to take them out of my hands and You make it for me. You bring the turmoil to an end, but don't let me waste my life, my time, or my energy where it will not be reciprocated if that is not Your will. Close the wrong doors, and only keep the right door open. If You are leading me away from this, then let Your favor bless me with opportunity, open doors, and provision to make change possible. Take me by the hand and lead me into the changes that You know are best. In Jesus name, amen.

Prayer to Overturn Injustice

Dear Heavenly Father,

You are able to do exceedingly, abundantly greater than anything I can ask or imagine, according to the power working within me. I ask You, Father, to cut a path through the enemy's controversies and outwit his entire scheme. You know the things that have been done to me unjustly. You see everything. You know what has motivated others to do what they do. I pray that you would outwit the liar, the fraud, the opportunist, the flatterer, the heavy handed oppressor, and the selfish heart. Break through into the life of those that do not fear You. You are the rider on the white horse, Lord Jesus, the Lord of the armies of angels; You carry the banner of my victory!

Ride into the battle, Lord Jesus, and pull every hidden thing out of darkness. The enemy only has power when he is cloaked in darkness and hides what he does. Uncover the darkness and shine Your light upon deception, ungodly motives and hidden agendas. Deliver those that are trapped, deceived, tormented and in bondage to the enemy. As an ambassador of Your Kingdom, I say, 'Let Your kingdom come and Your will be done, on earth as it is in heaven. Let the hand of the Lord be released against the powers of darkness and evil. Let the strong arm of the Lord be released against the works of the enemy.'

I ask You to unravel the enemy's plans. Set the stage for him to fall into his own trap and for wrong judgments to be overturned.

Your promise to me is, 'No weapon formed against me shall prosper and every tongue which rises up in judgment shall be refuted according to Isaiah 54:17.' Father, help me not to despise those that have been used by the enemy to hurt me. I choose to forgive them, but please do not leave me at the hands of those that despise me. I bless those that have treated me poorly and ask that You set them free from whatever is causing them to do the things they have done. Holy Spirit, I ask You to convict those that need to repent so that they may escape the evil one, be forgiven and healed. Lord, please set them free from, bitterness, fear, envy and jealousy. Set them free from murderous intent in their heart. Set them free from the wickedness that is allowing them to be pawns of the enemy. Heal and restore their soul. Let them find You.

Your word in Psalm 41:11 tells me that You uphold me in my integrity so that the enemy cannot shout in triumph over me. Psalm 20:6 says the LORD gives victory to his anointed. He answers him from his heavenly sanctuary with the victorious power of his right hand. Father, please answer this prayer and overturn the injustice has been done towards me. According to Your word in Psalm 63:11 and Psalm 31:18, shut the mouth of those that speak lies against me. I ask that Your Holy Spirit reveal truth in such a way that it overturns injustice. Explode into the lives of Your people, Lord Jesus; explode into the lives of Your enemies, and turn the conspiracies against your people upside down. What the enemy has intended for evil, now turn it around for good. Let a new judgment be issued from the court of heaven that declares me 'Not Guilty.' I believe You are able. Please restore my losses, I pray. In Jesus name, amen.

Prayer for a Creative Solution

Dear Heavenly Father,

I am stuck. I don't know what to do. I thank You that my lack of understanding can be solved through Your creativity. Father, You know everyone by name. You already know who You have chosen to help me through this dilemma. The wisdom that I lack, You have put in others. You are not limited by my limitations. Help me to understand that I must approach this situation with faith and not negativity. Open my mind to possibilities. Do not let me be pessimistic about thoughts and suggestions that I do not think will work. Instead, help me to have an attitude that gives the benefit of the doubt and makes room for You to move. Press me to follow through with the things You know You want me to do.

Please speak to others on my behalf and put my name and situation before them. Help them listen to their heart as You speak to them and direct them to assist me in my time of need. Bless them, Lord, for being willing to help me. Give them abundance so that they have no lack. I believe I can help give back to them as well, so help me to know what they need and how I can be of service to repay their kindness.

I ask You to please let Your favor help me in the things that I do not know how to do for myself. Holy Spirit, help me to be sensitive to Your directions and to recognize the form in which You are communicating to me. I ask for supernatural guidance to lead me to the right people that can help. I ask You to give me the creative ideas and inspired thoughts that are anointed for breakthrough. Help me to have the faith and the courage to follow through on whatever You show me, even if it does not make sense in the natural. Help me to know what doors to knock on and what to ask for. When I ask, let me receive a 'yes' from those that You have selected to come to my aid. Help me to hear You clearly, and not expect more from others than what they can give. Father, I thank You that if the right door doesn't exist, You can create it for me. Please form the door, create the solution, and lead me today to the person that has the missing piece of the puzzle that I need right now. I thank You for leading me to the solution that You know is right for me. Thank You, Lord, for creating a custom made solution for me. In Jesus name, amen.

Prayer for Those in Captivity

Father,

I am struggling to accept my situation. I honestly don't know how to accept where I am at right now. My heart is broken and I feel like You are so far away. I need You, Lord Jesus. You are the bridge between where I am at right now and my future. When I think of my future sometimes it feels completely hopeless, and I feel helpless to change it. Please take my brokenness and fill me with more of your Holy Spirit.

The only thing I can do right now is surrender myself into Your hands. In Jeremiah 29:11 Your word says that You have plans to do me good, to give me a future and a hope. I pray that You would lead me step by step into the plans You have for me. I have no idea what Your plans are, but help me to cling to this hope. Give me strength and courage to recover my faith, and truly believe that You do have a plan for me. Help me find peace in my present situation. Show me whatever it is You want me to learn. I pray that when I am tempted, You would help me to resist the things that can lead me into sin. Help me to choose righteousness over compromise. Give me eyes to see when the enemy is baiting the hook, trying to set me up. Give me extra grace and self control at those times, and help me use wisdom to avoid his snares.

I ask that Your Holy Spirit would comfort me and encourage me every day. Help me to have the discipline to read Your word and find encouragement in the scriptures. Help me to hear You and to recognize the form in which You communicate. The enemy wants to destroy my hope, but I am making a choice to take You at Your word. You said in Psalm 25:3 that no one that puts their hope in You will be put to shame. Help me to use this time to get to know You better, to learn Your ways, so that my faith can increase. Help me to love You right where I'm at. I pray that You help me find a sense of purpose and fulfillment even if I must remain in captivity for a while longer. Please break this yoke of heaviness and restore my joy so that my spirit can be free. I cannot get through this without joy, Lord.

I give You permission to change my heart and the way I view my situation. Please give me the change of heart that is necessary to see me through the dark days. You can change any situation in a moment, so I ask You to please work in my life to rearrange the things that need to change, and to create situations that will show me Your favor working on my behalf. I thank You for preparing me for Your good plans so that I am ready for them when the time is right. In Jesus name, amen.

Prayer for Terminal Health Conditions
Verses for Healing and Restoration

There is nothing more powerful than God's declared word. If you or a loved one is struggling in any area of life, begin to speak out the word of God. You must TURN the circumstances by declaring what GOD HAS SAID. Declaring God's word creates momentum to turn a situation in a new direction!

There is life in the word and scripture says it is also healing to our bodies. Proverbs 3:8 says, "This will bring health to your body and nourishment to your bones." God's Word IS His medicine. Isaiah 55:10, 11 says the Word of God will accomplish what it was sent out to do. The Word itself contains the power to produce what it says, but we have to RETURN the word to God by our spoken word. When we do, angels are listening so that they can be released on assignment to carry out the fulfillment of the word of God. (see Psalm 103:20).

Use this as a guide to declare over your own life or that of loved ones! Come into agreement with God's word and declare this: *'I have received the power of the Holy Spirit to lay hands on the sick and see them recover, to cast out demons, and to speak with new tongues. I have power over all the power of the enemy, and nothing shall by any means harm me.'* (Mark 16:17-18; Luke 10:17-19). Now, with **confidence**, declare: *'Those who I am praying for will recover fully and nothing by any means shall harm them in Jesus name!'*

I declare over (***Insert the name of the person you are praying for***):

- "No weapon formed against you shall prosper and any tongue that rises up against you shall be refuted for this is your inheritance in the Lord," according to Isaiah 54:17.
- "God will redeem your soul from the power of the grave, for He shall receive you," according to Ps. 49:15.
- "The Lord has caused you to live," according to Psalm 119:25.
- "The Lord has come to give you abundant life," according to John 10:10.

I declare,

- "Our God is the God of salvation; and to God the Lord belong escapes from death."
- "God has provided a way of escape from death for you," according to His word in Ps. 68:20.
- You have remembered the word to Your servant, upon which You have caused us to hope. This is comfort in our affliction, for YOUR WORD HAS GIVEN _____ LIFE." (Ps. 119:49,50)
- "O Lord, revive _____ according to Your justice." (Ps. 119:149)

- "Your tender mercies have come and cause _____ to live..." (Ps. 119:77)
- "By the stripes of Jesus you have been healed," according to Is. 53:5

I speak to your spirit and declare that you are...

- Complete in Him Who is the Head of all principality and power (Colossians 2:10).
- Alive with Christ, (Ephesians 2:5).
- Free from the law of sin and death, (Romans 8:2).
- Far from oppression, and fear does not come near you, (Isaiah 54:14).
- Born of God, and the evil one does not touch you, (1 John 5:18).
- Holy and without blame before Him in love, (Ephesians 1:4; 1 Peter 1:16).
- You have the mind of Christ, (1 Corinthians 2:16; Philippians 2:5).
- You have the peace of God that passes all understanding, (Philippians 4:7).
- You have the Greater One living in you; greater is He Who is in you than he who is in the world, (1 John 4:4). Let the One who is GREATER rise up in Jesus name!

- You have received the gift of righteousness and you reign as a king and priest through Jesus Christ, (Romans 5:17).
- You have received the spirit of wisdom and revelation in the knowledge of Jesus, the eyes of your understanding being enlightened, (Ephesians 1:17-18).

I declare to you (**insert name**),

- 'You have put off the old man and have put on the new man, which is renewed in the knowledge after the image of Him Who created you,' according to Colossians 3:9-10.
- 'You have no lack for your God supplies all of your need according to His riches in glory by Christ Jesus,' (Philippians 4:19). 'You have no lack in your health, in your life, in your faith, in your mental health, because Jesus Christ is the living word of God and He cannot lie. He has declared in Psalm 23:1 that He is your shepherd and you shall not lack. Therefore, whatever your need is, it has already been provided. I lay hold of it for you, on your behalf. Let your needs be filled according to the word of God in Psalm 23:1. I command it to come to you now, in Jesus name.

- 'You can do all things through Christ Jesus.' (Philippians 4:13).

- 'You will show forth the praises of God Who has called you out of darkness into His marvelous light,' (1 Peter 2:9).

- 'You are God's child for you are born again of the incorruptible seed of the Word of God, which lives and abides forever,' (1 Peter 1:23).

- 'You are God's workmanship, created in Christ unto good works,' (Ephesians 2:10).

- 'You are a new creature in Christ,' (2 Corinthians 5:17).

- 'You are more than a conqueror through Him Who loves you,' (Romans 8:37).

- 'You are an over comer by the blood of the Lamb and the word of your testimony,' (Revelation 12:11).

- 'You are a partaker of His divine nature,' (2 Peter 1:3-4).

- 'You are an ambassador for Christ,' (2 Corinthians 5:20).

- 'You are forgiven of all your sins and washed in the Blood,' (Ephesians 1:7).

- 'You are called of God to be the voice of His praise,' (Psalm 66:8; 2 Timothy 1:9).

- 'You are healed by the stripes of Jesus,' (Isaiah 53:5; 1 Peter 2:24).

- 'You are raised up with Christ and seated in heavenly places,' (Ephesians 2:6; Colossians 2:12).
- 'You are greatly loved by God,' (Romans 1:7; Ephesians 2:4; Colossians 3:12; 1 Thessalonians 1:4).
- 'You are strengthened with all might according to His glorious power,' (Colossians 1:11).

Father,

I ask You to judge this case in the court of heaven. The blood of Jesus speaks on behalf of (insert name of individual). Take the enemy to the court of heaven and Lord Jesus, plead their case against this ungodly foe. I plead the blood of Jesus upon any unbroken curses that might be hanging over _____ in the spirit realm. Cause him/her to live according to the sacrifice Jesus paid on behalf of us all. You are a just judge. Thank you for making the destroyer repay and restore what he has taken. I stand in the gap and make intercession for _____. The keys of death and Hades do not belong to the enemy, Father. You have given them to us, and I do not relinquish the keys to Satan. I ask You to rebuke the death angel and not let this life be cut short. It is not the enemy's rightful place to take his/her life. Thank you for restoring _____, even greater than before. Let angels be released to carry out the words of Your promises. In the name and authority of Jesus Christ Your Son I pray. Amen.

Prayer to Restore Proper Brain Function

Father God,

I thank You for Your Holy Spirit that gives us wisdom to know what to ask for in prayer. I pray for myself and ask You to send the answer to prayer. (You can also pray this over others, just substitute the word 'me' for the person's name).

I renounce fear, depression, anxiety, and compulsive behaviors. I renounce and repent for any ways I have come into agreement with the enemy. I thank You Jesus for your forgiveness and restoration. I believe You are the Son of God and You can heal me. You took my sin and disease upon yourself so that I could live victoriously. Please help me live freely. Let faith rise up in me and Your Holy Spirit fill me with wholeness, power and the fullness of God.

I ask that You would heal the cerebral cortex in my brain. I ask that You would fill any areas of deficiency with the fullness of Your Holy Spirit. Let the brain chemicals of serotonin, noradrenalin, norepinephrine, epinephrine, dopamine and all chemicals produced by the brain be correctly balanced. Let every deficiency be filled and every oversecretion be reduced to just the right levels for each individual. Let there be no overproduction of cortisol. Let every amino acid neurotransmitter function with perfect wholeness and soundness as it is in Jesus Christ. Let every gene that carried defective or mutated DNA that would perpetuate weakness, compromised health, mental instability or that which carries the result of a curse be healed at the cellular level. Infuse every cell, every gene, every strand of DNA with the DNA and healing of Jesus Christ. Let every curse be broken and sent back to the source, for You, O God did not give me any DNA that would carry a curse. It came from the evil one, and as I submit to Your authority, I resist the devil and command him to take back everything that he has brought upon me.

I pray that any damage to the brain itself, the neurotransmitters, and the centers for impulse control in the cerebral cortex be healed now in Jesus name. Let there be light in every darkened area of the brain, thought patterns and emotional responses. I declare the amino acid and peptide neurotransmitters be rewired to function in perfect health and send the proper amounts of chemicals to regulate impulse control, stress management, peace, pleasure and pain management in perfect balance. Let the acetylcholine functions be healed and restored to perfect health. Let the chemical agents and the communication messengers between brain cells function in perfect harmony, balance and soundness in every cell. Let all things in the molecular structure that affect mood, anxiety, appetite, sleep, temperature, heart rate, self control, discernment, impulse control, aggression, fear, stress management and other physical and psychological appetites, desires and occurrences be healed and restored to the perfect wholeness that exists in Jesus Christ.

Holy Spirit, let Your fullness fill my lack, for it is written, "the Lord is my Shepherd and I shall have no lack," according to Ps. 23:1. Let all areas that have been damaged, those areas that are genetically unsound, weak, impaired or afflicted be healed, for it is written, "Surely He has borne our griefs and carried our sorrows; yet we esteemed Him stricken, smitten by God and afflicted. But He was wounded for our transgressions, He was bruised for our iniquities, the chastisement for our peace was upon Him, and by His stripes we are healed," in Is. 53:4, 5.

Lord Jesus, You told us, Your disciples, to lay hands on the sick and they would recover, (Mark 16:18). You said in John 14:7 and again in John 14:16 that if we abide in You, we could ask whatever we desire in Your name and Your Father would do it, because it would bring glory to Your name. So I ask that I would be healed in the cellular, molecular level of my genes, in my DNA, and that anything that resides there that is not of Your placement, nor Your will be supernaturally removed, replaced with Your fullness and restored to perfect health right now, in Jesus name. Holy Spirit, please give me a revelation of my heavenly Father's love and acceptance so that perfect love will cast out all fear. Reveal my Father's heart towards me. Show me my truest identity as it is in Christ. Lead me to the salvation that is through Jesus Christ. I thank You and give You glory for the healing that is taking place now in Jesus name. Amen.

Prayer for Healing from Cancer

Dear Heavenly Father,

I know that cancer does not come from You. It comes from the pit of hell, but You overcame all the power of hell when You rose from the cross. The Bible says that YOU took the keys of death and Hades away from the enemy! You took the sin of all mankind and every evil thing upon Yourself. You were beaten - for us. Your word in Isaiah 53:5 declares this truth and that by Your stripes, we are healed. You would not have written it in Your word unless You meant what You said. So today, Lord, I say a prayer for _____, asking that you heal their body. Please fill them with the fullness of Your Holy Spirit and let the wholeness, the power and the peace that is in You manifest within them.

You have given Your children Your authority, and as Your child I command cancer to be placed upon the stripes You took on behalf of: (insert the name of the person you are praying for). I bind the spirits of infirmity, death and hell and forbid them from advancing against them in Jesus name. Spirit of death, flee _____ now! Spirit of Life, infuse _____ with resurrection life, strength, and perfect soundness. Jesus, You are the resurrection and the life! I command the root of this cancer and these tumors to wither and die immediately. Let salvation come to _____ now. Give him/her room to breathe, room for their organs to work properly, and room for life to flow unhindered in their body. I command the blood supply that feeds these tumors to cease. I command the cancer cells that reproduce uncontrollably to be supernaturally restrained and healed. Let all the healthy cells refuse to let cancer attach to them. Let the DNA of Jesus' perfect blood heal any areas that are predisposed to cancer. Let the broken spirit be healed, and the bones filled with fatness. I ask that the bone marrow be healed and filled with new, healthy red blood cells that continue to multiply exponentially. Let joy and laughter come back to _____ as their strength, for Your word says it is medicine to the body. We command all cancerous cells to leave _____ body now in Jesus name.

Father, I thank You for hearing these prayers and releasing Your answer into this earthly realm. I thank You that You are faithful to watch over Your word in order to bring Your promises to pass. Thank you for releasing healing. In Jesus name, amen.

Note: We have personally noticed the connection between physical disease such as cancer and unresolved unforgiveness and bitterness. The body often manifests the physical symptoms of a spiritual reality. That is one factor why some people do not get healed or perhaps they do get healed only to have it return. If the root of the spiritual issue has not been dealt with the problem can return. I am not saying this is true in every case, but there is a lot of evidence between unbroken curses, spiritual issues and physical disease.

Please ask the Lord if there is something that you need to specifically address in prayer to insure that your victory is 100%!

Prayer to Help With Forgiveness

Father God,

I thank You for showing me anyone I might still need to forgive. Bring their name to mind right now. I want to please You, so I ask for a gift of Divine Grace to be poured out into my heart. I ask You to enable me to see those that have hurt or offended me through Your eyes. Help me to see them through eyes of compassion so that I can truly forgive and be healed. My spirit is willing, Lord, but I know that sometimes I have a difficult time with my heart. I don't want to be stuck. Holy Spirit, I give You permission to change my perspective so that I can be obedient to You and forgive those that have hurt and disappointed me. Help me to recover my joy, Lord, for it is joy that becomes my strength to overcome. Help me to recover peace and experience Your presence in a greater way. Forgive me Lord, for I need Your forgiveness and Your mercy every day. In Jesus name, amen.

Prayer to Heal Sight

Father God,

I thank You for Your Holy Spirit that gives us wisdom to know what to ask for in prayer. I come to you in the name and authority of Jesus Christ, Your Beloved Son. I know You are a God of mercy, Lord Jesus, and You are able to heal. I know that whatever you ask from Your Father He will give you. You are the resurrection and the life, Lord, and I lift up (_____) ,(insert name of person you are praying for) to You right now in prayer.

I ask that You would fill any areas of (his/her) body that may have deficiencies, with the fullness of Your Holy Spirit, for it is written the Lord is our Shepherd and we shall have no lack, according to Ps. 23:1. I specifically speak to the brain, the spinal cord, the nerve conductors, and the eyes.

Let the brain chemicals of seratonin, noradrenalin, norepinephrine, epinephrine, dopamine and all chemicals produced by the brain be correctly balanced. Let every deficiency be filled and every over secretion be reduced to just the right levels for their body. Let every amino acid neurotransmitter function with perfect wholeness and soundness as it is in Jesus Christ. Let every gene that has carried defective or mutated DNA that would perpetuate weakness, compromised health, mental instability or that which carries the result of a curse be healed at the cellular level.

I pray that any damage to the brain itself, the neurotransmitters, and the centers for impulse control in the cerebral cortex be healed now in Jesus name. Let there be light in every darkened area of the brain, emotions and in their spirit man. I declare the amino acid and peptide neurotransmitters be rewired to function in perfect health and send the proper amounts of chemicals to regulate impulse control, stress management, peace, pleasure and pain management in perfect balance. Let the acetylcholine functions be healed and restored to perfect health. Let the chemical agents and the communication messengers between brain cells function in perfect harmony, balance and soundness in every cell. Let all areas that have been damaged, those areas that are genetically unsound, weak, impaired or afflicted be healed, for it is written, "Surely He has borne our grief and carried our sorrows; yet we esteemed Him stricken, smitten by God and afflicted. But He was wounded for our transgressions, He was bruised for our iniquities, the chastisement for our peace was upon Him, and by His stripes we are healed," in Is. 53:4, 5. Lord Jesus, You told us, Your disciples, to lay hands on the sick and they would recover, (Mark 16:18). You said in John 14:7 and again in John 14:16 that if we abide in You, we could ask whatever we desire in Your name and Your Father would do it, because it would bring glory to Your name. I command illness and disease to be removed and for their body to be healed in the name and authority of Jesus Christ.

I speak now to the eyes. I command the layers of tissue at the back of the eye to be filled with resurrection life in Jesus name. I command the choroid tissue to be filled with oxygenated blood and nourishment and for the retina to be securely fixed to the retinal wall. Let all the veins and capillaries that feed blood to the retina and the retinal wall open up and flow with oxygen rich blood that sustains healthy tissue development. I command all debris in the blood stream and those particles that might be lodged behind the eye to be supernaturally removed now. Let any holes or leaks in the vitreous gel-like substance of the eye be healed. Put a patch over the leak, Lord. Let there be new growth of healthy cells and tissue. If there is any collection of vitreous liquid under the eye, then supernaturally let it be removed and replaced back where it belongs, to provide a proper amount in the appropriate place in the eye. I command all shrinkage and contraction of muscles, tissue, ligaments, and the vitreous substance to cease now and for proper amounts to be maintained for healthy function of the eye, in Jesus name. I speak to the sclera, the cornea, the anterior and posterior chambers, the iris, the lens, the retina and vitreous humor, the rods and cones, the optic nerves and optic disk, the macula and the photoreceptors; I speak healing, restoration and recovery of sight in every area where it has been impaired or lacking. Let the rods and cones be of normal length, size and function. Whatever has been missing, even color cones, let them be restored now. I command all abnormal blind spots, or those that came as a result of injury, illness, trauma, disease or placed there by the enemy to be removed now, in Jesus name. I command all shadows or curtains over the eye to be removed now and for correct vision to be restored. I command each part of the eye to function as it was designed to function in God's perfect will. Let every injury, defect or the result of trauma, illness or disease be supernaturally reversed now, in the name and authority of Jesus Christ.

Father God, Lord Jesus, and Holy Spirit, I thank you for hearing my prayer and responding to it quickly. I know that all healing comes from You and I thank you for releasing healing for those I've prayed for, in Jesus name, Amen.

Prayer for God to Rescue and Deliver A Loved One

Father God,

Your word in Isaiah 59:1 says that Your arm is not too short to save, neither is Your ear dull so that You cannot hear. Your word tells me in Zephaniah 3:17 that You are mighty to save. I lift up (insert name of person you are praying for) to You, Lord. He/She needs a mighty deliverance.

Only You can see where they are at in their heart and in their life. I pray that You would cause their circumstances to change in such a way that it causes their will to line up with Your will and they call on Your name to be saved. Holy Spirit, put the name of Jesus Christ on their lips. Give them the seed of faith to call out to you.

If they are in trouble or need someone to physically help them, I ask You to send help right away. Even if they are unable to speak, I pray, send help immediately, Father. Send Your angels to rescue and deliver the ones who are lost, held captive against their will, or chained by the enemy. You alone know where to find those who are lost. Send help now, without delay!

I declare that the ears that have been dull and without understanding, those that have sought comfort through denial, and those that have been under a spirit of stupor are opened now, in the name and authority of Jesus Christ, according to Mark 7:35. Lord Jesus, you said in Isaiah 61:1 of your word, "The Spirit of the Lord GOD is upon *me,* because the LORD has anointed me to bring good news to the poor; he has sent me to bind up the brokenhearted, to proclaim liberty to the captives, and the opening of the prison to those who are bound;"

Therefore,

- I declare that every agreement (_____) has made with the enemy or works of darkness is unraveling now in the name and authority of Jesus Christ.
- I declare that (_____), my family and those in my city have turned back to You, O God, that they may be healed.
- I command the deaf ears to be opened now in the name and authority of Jesus Christ.
- I command the dullness to come out of people's hearts, and I declare they have been given a spirit of understanding from Your Holy Spirit, according to Matt. 13:15 and Is. 11:2.
- I break the spirit of stupor and release clarity, focus, and healing to people's minds. I declare that Your words are clear to them according to Mark 7:14.
- I declare that (_____), my family members, and those in my city hear the word of the Lord and are compelled to do what You instruct them to do, according to Acts 10:33.
- I declare that (_____) will give up their worldly desires and pursue the Lord Jesus Christ, according to Mark 8:34.
- I declare (_____) will confess the Lord Jesus Christ and be saved, according to Romans 10: 9,10.
- I declare that false brethren and lying signs and wonders will not deceive those who are called to be saved nor will they

turn them from the way of righteousness, according to Mark 13:22.

- I declare the spirit and power of repentance is released now to make (_____) ready to turn his/her heart back to their heavenly Father, according to Luke 1:17 and Malachi 4:6.

- I declare that (_____) has cried out to the Lord for his/her deliverance and salvation, and the Lord has saved them from all their distress. He has brought them out of darkness and the shadow of death, and has broken their chains in pieces, according to Ps. 107. 13, 14.

- I declare (_____) and others I am praying for are no longer dead in their trespasses but they have been revived according to Eph. 2:1.

- I declare that those I am praying for have turned away from their wickedness according to Acts 3:26.

- I declare (_____) my family, and those in my city have confessed their sins and received cleansing for their unrighteousness according to 1 John 1:9.

- I declare people have confessed their sins one to another so that they can be healed, according to James 5:16.

- I declare the generational curse of unbelief is broken according to Malachi 4:6.

- I declare our land, families and our cities are healed according to 2 Chronicles 7:14.

- I declare and decree that people will be found watching and waiting for Jesus Christ according to Luke 8:40.
- I declare that Jesus will find great faith according to Luke 7:9.
- I declare restoration is released according to Ezekiel 36:29-36.
- I declare the waste places are rebuilt and the breach has been repaired, according to Is. 58:12.
- I declare rivers of joy are flowing in dry places, according to Jer. 31:9 and Is. 41:18.
- I declare the head of the serpent that causes spiritual deafness is cut off, in the mighty name of Jesus Christ our Lord. Amen.

Prayer to Heal Depression

Father God,

I lift up those who are struggling with oppression, grief, depression and discouragement. I pray for as well as my family members, those in my workplace, neighborhood, community, and city of _____. I am anointed to console those who mourn and give them beauty for ashes, (Is. 61:3). Father, I know that joy comes from service to others, so today I ask for the opportunity to share my own testimony of how you comforted me. Bring someone to me where I have a personal experience that they can relate to, and let Your Holy Spirit bring the conversation up so that I have an opportunity to share about You. Hit the pause button so that there are no interruptions while You give me a chance to minister to the person You bring across my path. Give me Your words, Your love and the grace to speak to whomever You know needs my testimony or Your words of encouragement. I am just Your vessel, Lord. I yield to you. Fill my mouth with Your words and give me boldness to speak when the opportunity is presented. I command the spirits of fear, insecurity, unbelief, double mindedness, heaviness and discouragement to be broken now, in Jesus name! Let a spirit of faith and forgiveness come upon them now in Jesus name! Holy Spirit, I ask that You convict people where they need to change so that they may recover their joy.

I declare that because I love righteousness and hate wickedness, therefore my God has anointed me with the oil of gladness more than my companions. (Ps. 45:7). I am anointed to give others the oil of gladness in exchange for their mourning, and give them the garments of praise for the spirit of heaviness, according to Is. 61:3.

I bind the spirit of heaviness from all who cross my path. When I walk into a room, across the street, through the parking lot, into my office, into a restaurant or wherever I go, I declare that the spirits of fear, anxiety and heaviness are bound in the name of Jesus and rendered paralyzed, impotent and powerless. A spirit of joy and gladness will unexpectedly overtake those that are in my presence. I release it into the atmosphere now and ask that Holy Spirit overflow the joy of the Lord upon anyone I encounter. Let rivers of joy flow in dry places! Let rivers of living water flow in their innermost being, according to John 7:38. For it is written, "If anyone thirsts, let them come to Me and drink. He who believes in Me, as the scripture has said, 'out of his heart shall flow rivers of living water. "

I declare the joy of the Lord to be our strength, and will overtake others in my presence. Your word says laughter is like good medicine. Let your joy and laughter break out unexpectedly and be medicine to the souls of those around me. There is joy unspeakable and the glory of the Lord in Your presence, and I declare a release of Your presence into the very atmosphere wherever I go, in Jesus name.

Prayer to Outwit the Enemy

Dear Holy Spirit,

I ask that you open my eyes to see into the unseen realm. Show me exactly what the enemy is doing and what his assignment is against me so that I know how to pray. Give me specific knowledge so that nothing catches me off guard. I ask for prophetic gifting and the gifts of the Spirit to be given to me. I ask for the gift of understanding dreams and visions. I ask for interpretation that will enable me to understand the spirit realm with clarity. Bless me by filling me with the fullness of your Holy Spirit. Baptize me in the Holy Spirit and let a fresh new anointing be poured out upon me. I love You, Holy Spirit, and I ask for sensitivity to help me know You better. I don't want to grieve You. If I have, forgive me. I ask for Your assistance to help me to outwit the enemy at every turn. Help me to see the snares the enemy would set and walk around them. Keep my feet out of the traps. Help me see when the enemy uses a baited hook to try to draw me in. Give me strength and the fruit of self control so that I can resist the enemy. Please bless me with the spirit of understanding so that I rightly discern the motivation of people's hearts. Let a spirit of understanding give me insight into the enemy's plans, and correctly discern what spirits are at work. Help me also to know the proper course of action regarding the things you reveal. In Jesus name, amen.

Prayer to Keep From Stumbling

Heavenly Father,

I ask You to guard and protect me. Keep me in the ways of righteousness, truth and integrity in every matter. Grant me revelation, wisdom and understanding that will alert me to the plots of the enemy and his subtle tactics of deception. Draw me away from temptations that would lead me into compromise and sin. Please do not allow me to be tempted more than I can bear. Show me the way of escape and help me to run to it. You know my weaknesses and limitations. Open my eyes to truth so that I am not blinded by pride in one particular area. Do not let the foot of pride cause me to be caught in a snare. Help me choose the path of humility and righteousness.

Help me not to neglect my marriage, family and other key relationships. Strengthen my family relationships so that the enemy cannot find anything to exploit. Remind me not to hold onto offense or grudges and to forgive others quickly. Help me to remember to pray for my loved ones daily, and to pray *with* them. Help me to build strong spiritual relationships with my family and to encourage one another daily.

Holy Spirit, help me not to embrace the things I should let go of. Help me not to entertain envy, jealousy, self-pity or emotional hurt. Heal me from all past hurts and brokenness. Guard me from making judgments about others when You have called me to love and show grace.

Help me to be full of Your Holy Spirit; to have my mind controlled, directed and fixed on God. Help me so that I do not get comfortable in worldliness. Instead, I pray that You consistently fan the flame within me and continue to create, over and over again, a passionate desire to pursue Your presence, towards prayer and a love for You. Help me not to think of myself more highly than I ought, and end up falling into error or corruption. Enable me to stand against the wiles of the enemy, but with grace and humility. Help me not to overstep my bounds and enter into another person's ministry office to which I am not called. Lord, help me to know my area of gifting and service and to do it diligently, but not to overstep and presumptuously enter into an area where I am not called. Help me, Lord, not to get so excited over the good things that You do for me that I end up taking the credit for it and claiming the glory for myself. When the enemy tempts me with pride and vainglory, immediately allow me to recognize the temptation, renounce it and put the enemy in his place, under my feet! I ask you to help me recognize the subtleties of the enemy's deception, to immediately take every thought that exalts itself above the knowledge of Christ into obedience, and cast down every vain imagination. I thank You, Holy Spirit, that you are able to keep me from stumbling and enable me to stand with You for righteousness sake. In Jesus name, amen.

Prayer to Declare the Blood of Jesus

There is POWER for PROTECTION. It was the shed blood of Jesus that won the victory on cross and defeated all the power of the enemy. What was true then is still true today. Declare the power of Jesus' blood over every aspect of your life!

- I declare the power of Jesus' blood is healing for every broken relationship, for the ministry of reconciliation is the ministry of Jesus Christ.
- I declare the power of Jesus' blood over offense, misunderstanding, unforgiveness and bitterness of past events.
- I declare the power of Jesus' blood to cleanse my heart and mind from toxic thoughts and emotions.
- I declare the power of Jesus' blood to cleanse and heal my body.
- I declare the power of Jesus' blood over strongholds and areas of unbelief. I command every stronghold to collapse and surrender to truth.
- I declare the power of Jesus' blood to remove unclean or impure desires.
- I declare the blood of Jesus cleanses my conscience from dead works, guilt and shame.
- I declare the blood of Jesus defeats lust and soulish ambitions.

- I declare the blood of Jesus triumphs over pride, rebellion, and stubborn resistance.
- I declare the blood of Jesus eradicates unloving thoughts and self hatred.
- I declare the blood of Jesus overcomes the spirit of rejection.
- I declare the blood of Jesus heals emotional brokenness and wounding.
- I declare the blood of Jesus supercedes accusation, judgment and religious attitudes.
- I declare the blood of Jesus protects me from wrong covenants.
- I declare the blood of Jesus protects my marriage and family.
- I declare the blood of Jesus guards and protects my home and family members.
- I declare the blood of Jesus rebukes the devourer from my life.
- I declare the blood of Jesus destroys oppression, depression, hopelessness and grief.
- I declare the blood of Jesus heals all my sickness and disease.
- I declare the blood of Jesus defeats death.
- I declare the blood of Jesus seals the doors of my past shut.
- I declare the blood of Jesus cleanses me from all unrighteousness.
- I declare the blood of Jesus covers the sins of me and my ancestors.
- I declare the blood of Jesus protects and preserves the doors of my future.

- I declare the blood of Jesus redeems and delivers my loved ones.

- I declare the blood of Jesus redeems me from every curse.

- I declare the blood of Jesus protects me from poverty and hopelessness.

- I declare the blood of Jesus compels God to intervene in my situation.

- I declare the blood of Jesus is a promise of His devotion and loving care in my life.

- I declare the blood of Jesus triumphs over all the power of the enemy.

- I declare the blood of Jesus raises a standard against the enemy.

- I declare the blood of Jesus compels Him to fight for my victory!

Prayer to Heal the Family Tree

Father God,

In the name and authority of Jesus Christ I come to you and ask that you give people everywhere the desire to heal their family tree. Give them a heart to search for the right answers and faith to take the appropriate actions that make that possible. I pray for my own family to be healed, and I pray for other families to be healed. Let the family tree that represents the family of God be healed as well.

Let eyes blinded by pride, prejudice, offense and accusation be opened now to see beyond those barriers. Help me, and help others to see the good and godly things in those that have been kept at a distance. Correct spiritual vision so that we can see what You see in people, Lord. Let ears that have been closed to truth be opened now, in Jesus name. Let people be willing to listen to one another.

Release your angels to anoint the ears to hear what Your Spirit is saying. Let hearts be softened to make room for relationships to be healed. Instead of looking for reasons to stay at a distance from others, help me to look for reasons to draw closer. Help my family members do the same, Lord. Help those in Your family, Father, to move towards healing and restoring relationships. I pray that we would all be willing to give others the benefit of the doubt, to think the best of others. Help us not to focus on our differences, but to find things that we can appreciate about one another. I ask that You supernaturally place that seed of love and desire for relationship in the hearts of those that You wish to knit together. Let anyone that feels stubborn or resistant have a sudden change of heart. Give them a willing desire to reconcile the relationships You want healed and restored. Let all stumbling blocks be supernaturally removed now, in Jesus name.

Father, let what has been broken through hurt, misunderstanding, betrayal, anger, offense, jealousy and broken trust be healed. Heal what has been torn by pride. Take those relationships that have been estranged from one another and make them whole again. Whether it is family members or members of Your body, heal and restore that which has been wounded and broken. Pour in Your love, grace, forgiveness and mercy. Pour a new foundation and restore the bonds of loyalty, trust and respect in Jesus name.

Lord, heal us all from our harshness and prejudices. Heal us from self righteous convictions and offenses that are not from You, and tend to keep us from fully accepting and being able to love others. Help us to let go of pride and other attitudes that makes us feel that others are not worthy of our acceptance. Lord, heal our memories. The enemy would try to rob us from the good memories. Restore to us the happy memories that give people a desire to see relationships healed.

Take what was once broken and heal those fractured areas. Heal disappointments and pour in Your grace. Give me compassion to see others through eyes of love and understanding, not hurt or judgment. I pray that the issues that once existed would become a non-existent thing. Remove the things that were once issues to divide us. Cement hearts together in covenant bonds that cannot be broken. Let Your Holy Spirit be the threefold cord binding hearts and lives together that is by the appointment and design of God, in Jesus name.

I declare and decree in the mighty name of Jesus Christ that the mark the enemy has placed upon the heads of your children must be supernaturally removed now. Let Your angels be released to remove those marks of rejection. Let every word curse be cancelled and negative words be condemned according to Your promise in Isaiah 54:17.

I thank You Father for hearing my prayer and sending out help from the sanctuaries of heaven and earth. May the family trees be healed according to Your desire, in Jesus name I pray. Amen.

Prayer for a Healthy Pregnancy

Father God,

I thank you that children are a blessing from the Lord. I stand before You today and declare YOU are faithful. I will enjoy the blessing of children for you have given me your promises.

Your word declares in Psalm 127:3 that the fruit of the womb is a reward and Psalm 128:3 also promises that I will have children that flourish like young olive plants in my home. I declare the blessing of Prov. 31 over myself and my womb, that the day will come when my husband and my children will rise up and call me blessed.

I declare according to Your promise in Exodus 23:26 that because I love you and serve You and worship You, O God, You will bless my provision; you will take sickness away from me and I will NOT suffer miscarriage or be barren. I will fulfill the number of my days, in Jesus name.

Father, I remind You of Your promise in Malachi chapter 3. I tithe and am a giver, Lord, and because of that, You have promised to rebuke the devourer for my sake. You promised that the devourer would not destroy the fruit of my ground and You said my vine would not fail to bear fruit in the field (vs. 11) so I thank You for fruitfulness to come forth from my womb and that the devourer is rebuked in Jesus name.

Lord, You also said in Job 22:28 that I would declare a thing and it would be established for me so that light would shine on my ways. I make this declaration now and ask You to establish this for me.

- I declare that my body is now and will continue to produce abundant levels of all hormones necessary to maintain a normal, healthy birth. I declare my progesterone levels are increasing exponentially daily and will continue to do so throughout my pregnancy.

- I declare that I will bring forth a healthy child out of my womb. I call for my child to come forth out of heaven and into my womb. I speak life into my uterus. I break the power of every negative word over my body, my family, my future, and children yet to come.

- I declare I will not experience placenta previa, leaking of amniotic fluid, premature miscarriage, pre-eclampsia, abnormal bleeding or any other complications.

- I declare that You have an appointed time for childbirth and I will not give birth before that appointed time.

- I declare that the placenta will adhere normally to the uterine wall.

- I declare that all cells will divide normally and each cell will produce healing and perfect soundness as it forms new life inside of me. I will not experience ectopic pregnancy, congenital defects, inherited disease or other abnormalities. If it is not allowed in heaven, I do not receive it. There is no disease in heaven, Father. I resist those things and declare all possible inherited generational curses broken now in Jesus name.

Father, please forgive anyone in our family line that may have neglected to ask Your forgiveness for their sins. Forgive, I pray, sins of broken covenants, broken trust, idolatry, rebellion and any ungodly covenants that may have been made. Let them be broken now in Jesus name. Please forgive any inherited generational iniquitous sin and let the blood of Jesus be applied to those sins. I declare that I am a new creation in Christ and there is life in the blood. I thank You, Lord Jesus that Your DNA flows through me to make me whole and complete in every way. I thank You for your Holy Spirit that is full of life, strength and power. Let the perfect soundness and wholeness that is in Your Spirit flow through me and release healing throughout my body. I declare no curse will pass through the blood of Christ. I submit to Your Lordship in my life and I resist the power of evil. I refuse it and declare it will not come near me. I thank You Father for continuing to show me how to pray specifically as I believe for a healthy pregnancy. In Jesus name, amen.

Prayer to be Delivered from Sexual Sins (and Sexual Demons)

Father God,

I need a Savior, a Deliverer. Lord Jesus, I believe you paid the price for my sin *and shame* when you went to the cross on my behalf. I do not have to bear the weight of it any longer. Jesus, I pray that Your blood would wash over my mind, my body and my spirit and make me clean. Renew in me a pure thought life. I come to you to ask you for healing from lust, perverse spirits and demonic attachments of incubus and succubus spirits. I take responsibility for the things I've done, the things I've allowed, and even things that have been done to me against my will. Right now I forgive _____ (speak the names of those that have sinned against you) so that I can also have my own sins forgiven, and I ask You to empower me to do so. As a matter of my will, I choose to forgive them and ask that You, Father, give me grace and strength to not take this offense back into my heart. I ask that You heal those that have perpetrated sins against me, and set us free from the perversity and sin that has had us bound. Lord Jesus, I give myself to You and ask that You forgive my sin. Please forgive the sin of my family and ancestors. Forgive all the ways that we all rejected You and rebelled against your ways, and exerted our independence from You. Forgive idolatry, witchcraft, involvement with the occult, shedding innocent blood, broken vows and covenants. Forgive the many things we have done to deny Your Lordship. Let Your blood cover our sins, I pray. Be

Lord of my life. I take You as my Savior, Master, Husband, Friend, and Lord. I will not have any other gods besides You. I make a covenant with You, Jesus. Help me to be faithful to You. Thank you, Father, for accepting me and adopting me into the kingdom of God.

Satan, you *are not* my husband or my master. I *renounce* you. *I divorce you.* I want nothing to do with you ever again. I reject your seed and your lies. I reject, refuse, renounce and **divorce** all unclean demonic spirits of perversity including incubus, mare and succubus spirits, spirits of lust, pornography, pedophilia, voyeurism, domination, brutality, homosexuality, confusion, gender confusion, astral projection and spirit travel, mischievous and trouble-making spirits, spirits of double-mindedness, unbelief, sodomy, rape, anger, rage, bitterness, unforgiveness, witchcraft, lust, idolatry, hard heartedness, accusation, familiar and familial spirits, pride, rebellion, and death. I renounce and divorce Lilu and Lilith, and all the offspring that comes from Satan and his demons. If there is anything unclean of Satan's seed implanted within me, I command it to shrivel and die immediately in the name and authority of Jesus Christ. I repent for any ways that I have knowingly or unknowingly come into agreement with these spirits, and I humbly submit myself to the Lord Jesus Christ and the authority of His Holy Spirit.

I submit to You, O God, and I resist the enemy, commanding him to flee from me and take everything he has put on me, everything he has brought into my life, and *get out* in Jesus name! I reject every seed of Satan I command them to die immediately, in Jesus name. I curse Satan's seed and declare, "YOU WILL BEAR

NO MORE FRUIT EVER AGAIN," by the name and authority of Jesus Christ. His blood covers these sins and I command these doors to be shut, never to open again.

Let every cord of sin, shame, fear, witchcraft, and soul ties from ungodly sources be severed now, in Jesus name. I renounce the soul ties to former lovers, spouses, and others that may be tied to me in the spirit. Let any fragments of their souls return to them, and let any scattered and fragmented parts of my soul return to me, in Jesus name. Let all those that would practice astral projection, spirit travel, witchcraft or other occult practices against me find the door closed. Let there be blindness into this evil eye now. I bind and forbid the entrance of demonic spirits into my life in Jesus name, according to your promise in Matthew 18:18. What is bound on earth has already been bound in heaven.

I release myself from all shame, resentment, fear, insecurity and feelings of inferiority that have come upon me as a result of sexual molestation and other sins against my body - both those that were done without my consent, and those that I may have participated in - willingly or unwillingly. I reject and refuse all perverse spirits, lying spirits, familiar spirits, incubus and succubus spirits and Lust. I command them to go now back to the abyss in Jesus name. I bind the dark angel of the night known as Lilith, and the screech owl that brings terror by night in the name and authority of Jesus Christ. I forbid it to enter my life, that of my family or my home.

Let all evil trees be pulled up by the roots out of my life now in Jesus name. I command every spirit that does not worship Jesus Christ; every spirit that does not confess Jesus Christ has come in the flesh, and any spirit that does not declare Jesus Christ as Master to leave me and my household at once, in the name of Jesus.

I receive by faith the healing for my mind, my emotions, my body and spirit. I receive by faith the mind of Christ, and I choose this day to pull up the root of bitterness and replace it with the love of God. I ask You Lord to plant forgiveness, purity, obedience, peace, joy and love in place of bitterness. Fill me with Your Holy Spirit and let the spirit of adoption be poured out into my heart in Jesus name. Let your love and acceptance captivate my heart, O God.

You are transforming me, renewing my mind, to become the living word, as Your truth is lived out in me. You are transforming me to become the anointed of God. I am not a victim, I am victorious. I do not fear, the enemy is fearful of me. I declare that no weapon formed against me shall prosper, and every tongue that rises up against me is refuted according to Your word in Isaiah 54:17. I walk in the fullness of God, in Jesus name.

I thank you, Lord Jesus, for being my healer, restorer, redeemer and protector. I thank you for replacing every lie in my belief system with the truth that will set me free. Thank You, Holy Spirit for releasing revelation as to my true identity in Christ. Show me how You see me. Show me if I have believed lies about my true identity. I thank You for establishing and settling me in faith and truth, in Jesus name.

Help me, Lord Jesus, to identify and break free from any relationships that are unhealthy and undesirable in Your eyes. Help me to honor Your word, Your will and Your wishes. You know my weaknesses; I pray for strength to overcome them. For those things that You know I cannot or will not be able to overcome in my own strength, I pray that You would take them out of my hand. Let it be done according to Your will for my life and for the benefit of Your will carried out in the lives of others, too. Lord, replace those relationships with better ones that will strengthen me in my walk with you, and fill the void for love, relationship and friendship.

Father God, I thank You for overcoming victory. Please fill me with Your Holy Spirit and empower me to live for You. Help me to live a life that honors You and brings You glory. In Jesus name, amen.

Note: This prayer covers the topics of lust, pornography, sexual molestation, and problems with demonic spirits of incubus and succubus. This prayer also helps with sexual identity issues and gender confusion, as all the same spirits are involved. These demons are very persistent with their victims. I highly recommend fasting along with prayer.

Prayer to Break Generational Curses
Breakthrough Prayer
(This helps remove many blocks to prayer.)

Dear Heavenly Father,

Right now I declare that I break every agreement with Satan and the works of darkness. I choose this day to divorce the enemy, to renounce and repent of any covenants that have been made by me or other family members in my generational line. According to Your word in 2 Chronicles 7:14, Father, You said that if I would humble myself, pray and seek Your face...If I would turn and repent from my wicked ways, You said You would forgive my sins and heal my land. Whether I or other family members have partaken of these sins knowingly or unknowingly, I ask Your forgiveness and I renounce:

All spirits of fear, the fear of man that brings a snare, self pity, insecurity, and inferiority. Forgive those in my family line for the need to control or manipulate others out of a sense of fear, insecurity or inferiority. Forgive us for not trusting in your provision or your timing, and for failing to rest in Your love.

I renounce all spirits of heaviness that bring depression, mental illness, obsessive compulsive disorders, schizophrenia, suicide, and grief. I renounce the spirits of unbelief, double-mindedness, the cares of this world and all things that would give me give me divided loyalties in my heart and mind towards God. I renounce every seed that Satan has sown into my heart and mind that would cause divided loyalties and weaken my convictions towards Jesus Christ. I renounce bipolar disease and unbelief. I renounce all compulsive behavior and all addictions rooted in fear, rejection, or anxiety. I renounce self pity and the lie that I cannot or will not be healed. I renounce the tendency to think of myself as a victim or a martyr. Father, You love me and did not give me sickness, disease, torment or problems. Those came from the pit of hell. Jesus died for this truth and I will not reject Your truth. I reject the lies from the enemy and declare that I receive the truth and the healing that is afforded to me as a child of God, for it is written, "By His stripes, I AM healed," in Jesus name.

I renounce and forsake all spirits of discontent, complaining, a vagabond spirit, wandering and irresponsibility that have come from iniquity and idolatry. I renounce and forsake any sins and demonic spirits associated with gambling, poverty spirits, laziness and sins of poor stewardship. I renounce all addictive behaviors given to excess, greed or stinginess.

I renounce bitterness, jealousy, strife, anger, hatred, profanity, gossip, lying, slander and murder. I renounce the bitterness that comes from being hurt, mistreated or injustice that has occurred towards myself or others in my family. I renounce the spirit of Cain, which is a murderous spirit. I repent and forsake the sins of slander, hatred and evil speaking. I renounce the bitterness that comes from being hurt or mistreated, injustice towards me or others in my family. I repent of my judgments against others. Forgive me and those in my family for any sins of hard heartedness, being critical or condemning, or showing lack of compassion towards others in their time of need. Forgive me and those in my family line for turning a blind eye towards those in need and withholding good when it was in our power to help.

I renounce and forsake unforgiveness, including unforgiveness towards myself, retaliation, and vengeance. Forgive me, Lord, for any time that I or my family members have sown seeds of discord or caused pain to others through our actions. Forgive us for acts of maliciousness or things that me or other family members have done with the intent to hurt and cause pain to others. Forgive me and those in my family line for selective obedience or ignoring the prompting of your Holy Spirit when You wanted us to show love, mercy, grace or compassion.

I renounce and forsake the sins of pride, lawlessness, rebellion, selfish ambition, presumption, and testing God. I renounce and forsake atheism, mockery, scoffing the things of God and Your Holy Spirit, grieving the Holy Spirit and unbelief. Forgive me Lord, for allowing spirits of inferiority or insecurity to drive me to feel as though I have to prove myself to others, myself or to You. Forgive me for believing these lying spirits when they tried to form a false image in me. Your word says I am fearfully and wonderfully made, and I am made in Your image. I am accepted just as I am. Forgive me and my family line for despising godly wisdom and authority or rejecting Your counsel. Forgive us for self-rule and choosing authority figures that did not represent Your government or authority for our lives. I repent from any time that I have cursed God or others.

Forgive me Lord, for loving gossip, slander and my judgments more than I loved your law of showing love and kindness. Forgive me for not blessing others more freely. Forgive me for not being kind to others when I should have shown kindness.

I renounce and forsake all soul ties to illegitimate spiritual fathers or spiritual leaders, religious attitudes, and spirits of legalism, disrespect, self righteousness, prejudice, controlling behaviors, manipulation, imposing my will on others, racism, disobedience, independence, critical spirits, arrogance, vain and judgmental attitudes. I forgive everyone that has knowingly or unknowingly contributed to my hurt.

I renounce and forsake spirits of rejection and abandonment, all lying spirits and command them to leave me at once. I repent for sins of judging or rejecting others, withholding love, acceptance or forgiveness. I renounce and forsake spirits of self-hatred, self rejection, unloving spirits, guilt, unforgiveness and anger towards myself and others. I renounce the lie that sins done to me by others were my fault. I renounce the shame and condemnation that have come in as a result of deep wounds, embarrassment and sins that were done to me from others. I surrender my pain and anger and I want no benefit from it anymore. I surrender the memories of hurtful events in my life. Take it Lord, I offer it all to you right now. Help me not take it back! I forgive those individuals, Lord. I put them in your hands. Forgive me for not being able to separate the sin of those that have hurt me from them as human beings that have also been hurt and used by the enemy to hurt others. Forgive me for the times when I have not honored nor shown respect to those in authority, parents, spouses or others. Forgive me for not humbling myself or apologizing when I should have done so. Forgive me for broken relationships, broken vows and covenants, and please help me to do whatever I am responsible for to make things right. I ask You to heal the breach in relationship between myself, others and You.

I renounce and forsake all worldly addictions including drugs, alcohol, nicotine, gambling, gluttony, compulsive physical exercise, compulsive spending, sexual sins against myself and others, pornography, and sins of excess that feed the lusts of the flesh. I renounce and forsake the spirits of lust, bondage, pharmacia or drugs.

I renounce and forsake the spirit of pride and Leviathan. I renounce and forsake the perverse spirit and all that is connected to it. I renounce and forsake incubus and succubus spirits, spirits of voyeurism, homosexuality, beastiality and anything connected to demonic sex. I renounce and forsake unfruitful thoughts, fantasies, all unclean and seducing spirits, and the deceiving spirits connected to the perverse spirit. I renounce ungodly soul ties, those of former lovers, false authority figures, and soul ties to anyone that would keep me from moving out of my past and into the good future You have for me. Let those ties to the past be severed now, in Jesus name. I repent of all sexual sins. I renounce and forsake the strongman of Baal and divorce all ungodly spirits of lust, sex and witchcraft. Please heal the fragmentation in my soul and spirit.

I renounce and forsake all false gods and masters and all evil inheritances in my generational line. I renounce and repent, on behalf of myself and my ancestors for any covenants or agreements made with the seven African spirits known as Papa Legba, Obtala, Oya, Oshun, Chango, Ogun and Yemmaya. I declare there is no other God except for Jesus Christ and I break any connections or agreements that have been made through candle burning, calling on the names of false gods or saints, and invoking their assistance. I renounce all lies and false teaching that blinds me to truth and substitutes works for grace. I repent for any ways that I have mocked You. I renounce all ungodly symbols that connect me to false teaching, false gods, ungodly alliances and pagan symbolism.

I accept and receive no inheritance from evil sources, only that which my heavenly Father permits and allows. Let all evil inheritances be broken off of me and my family. I put them under the blood of Jesus. I renounce and forsake the spirit of mammon, greed, and selfishness. I renounce and forsake the divided loyalties that come with a love for money, covetousness, idolatry and envy. I renounce bitterness and the lie that I am not blessed by the Lord. I renounce the lie that I will be happier with more material possessions. I renounce the lie that somehow I am rejected or unworthy because I do not have more possessions. I renounce the sin of comparing myself with others.

I renounce and repent for any involvement with secret societies and the ungodly covenants they demand. (If you know which ones are involved in your family history, name them).I renounce and forsake all pledges, oaths and involvement with the Masonic Lodge and Freemasonry, Job's Daughters, Shriners, Illuminati, secret lodges, societies or crafts by my ancestors and myself. I renounce all false marriage covenants and mock ceremonies of secret societies. I renounce and forsake blasphemy and taking the Lord's name in vain, as well as blasphemous oaths, alliances and pledges to Satan by any other name. I renounce and forsake all witchcraft spirits. I renounce and forsake all practices and traditions of Santeria and Lucemi, and praying to false gods, saints and Orishas.

I renounce and forsake the Rosy Cross, the Rosicrucians and all ungodly alliances, oaths and associations to Grand Knights. I renounce and forsake all false gods of Egypt as well as the lust of power, prestige and position. I renounce and forsake all secret signs and handshakes. I renounce and forsake all false gods, false doctrines, unholy communion and abominations. I renounce and forsake the Luciferian doctrine; I renounce and forsake the oaths spoken to pledge loyalties to man or idol that violated the commands of God and conscience. I renounce all false masters associated with Freemasons, Shriners, Mormonism, Paganism, the Klu Klux Klan and other lodges and secret societies. I renounce and forsake the false god Allah. Forgive me for believing I have had to work to earn your love and approval. I renounce and forsake all words and phrases used as secret codes and I break agreement with all curses that were once agreed to be placed upon any and all family members, including myself and future generations. I renounce and forsake the compass point, the cable tow, the hoodwink, the ball and chain, the apron, the noose around the neck, the sword and spear, the blindfold and the mind blinding effect of those things. I renounce and forsake all penalties associated with breaking these ungodly oaths and covenants. I renounce and forsake all play acting and rituals depicting murder and death, and the spirit of fear associated with death as a curse. I revoke and break the power of agreement with these ungodly servants of darkness, Satanic worship, and all associations with those in fellowship of demonic alliances. I command the curse to be cancelled and all ungodly covenants and agreements broken and nullified both in the earthly and spiritual realm, in the name of Jesus Christ. I ask You, Father, Son and Holy Spirit to heal and restore every area of the physical body and ailments that have been suffered as a result of the curse brought on by any involvement by anyone in my family line. Forgive us, I pray, for committing sin and iniquity and blasphemous acts against a Holy God, ourselves and others.

I renounce, forsake and divorce myself from and break any and all agreements, covenants or involvement with: all lying spirits, the occult, demonic spirits, Native American and cultural rituals and traditions involving the use of idols, witchcraft, voodoo, the practice of hoodoo, root workers, witch doctors, conjuring, the practice of juju, black magic, white magic, Wicca, and the use of mediums, familiar spirits and seducing spirits. I renounce and forsake all oaths and rituals to false gods, witchcraft covens, sorcerers, Satanists or workers of iniquity. I renounce and forsake any and all sins involving the abuse of trust, authority, and power or using our influence in an ungodly manner. I renounce and forsake sins involving magic, sorcery, practicing charms or incantations, the use of horoscopes, tarot cards, fortune telling, astral projection, psychic energy or astrology. I will burn and destroy all books, spells, incantations, rings, and other objects that connect me to ungodly occult practices, lodges, secret societies or their unholy rituals and practices.

I bind any and all inanimate objects from being used in any sort of witchcraft, voodoo, hoodoo or other form of demonic practices and loose all evil spirits off of individuals, objects, and evil altars. I command them to go to the abyss that was created for them in Jesus name.

I renounce and forsake all spirits of divination, the spirit of Python, the Serpentine spirit and all that take the form of the demonic serpent. I renounce and ask Your forgiveness, Father, for speaking things in Your name, even prophesying, that has been out of the flesh rather than the unction of the Holy Spirit.

I renounce and repent for all broken covenants, unfulfilled vows and promises, betrayal and divorce. I ask You to please disentangle me and release me from ungodly covenants, vows, and peace treaties, and all unrighteous agreements that would bring me into relationships where I am unequally yoked with things of the kingdom of darkness, evil and wrong relationships. Lord, let there be a release of every curse that has come against me or my generational line as a result of these things. I decree a cancellation of every form of witchcraft and curse that has resulted from my involvement or that of my generational line. I ask You, Lord Jesus, to come and deliver me and my family from all demonic spirits that have come as a result of a curse. I ask that You deliver me and my family from every affliction, illness, disease, allergy, or physical condition that has affected us. I ask that You restore all the years that the enemy has stolen. Let finances, health, and relationships be restored. Let peace, joy, mental health and emotional stability be restored. Let the blessings that have been held back, stolen and hidden by the enemy be released into my hands now, in Jesus name. Let all demonic attachments be severed from me and my family line, both in the heavenly places as well as in the earthly realm. I declare that every seed that was sown by Satan in order to perpetuate a curse or cause myself or someone else in my family line to reject my heavenly Father, the Lord Jesus Christ and Holy Spirit must now shrivel and die immediately. Jesus, I give You permission to change what You know needs to change in my life and to convict me if I resist your Holy Spirit.

Your word says in Isaiah 54:17 that "No weapon formed against me shall prosper, and every tongue which rises up against me in judgment shall be condemned," and that this is my inheritance in the Lord. Right now I condemn every negative word that has been spoken over myself, my family and my future in Jesus name. I repent for speaking negative words and I condemn every negative word I have spoken over myself, my family, and our future. I declare they will not boomerang back into my life or theirs. I break the power of those negative words that hang in the spirit like a curse. I declare that words that have been used as a weapon will no longer ring in the ears of my loved ones and hinder their faith or their future in Jesus name. From this day forward, I declare their ears shall be deaf to condemning words and only faith shall prosper in their heart, mind and spirit in Jesus name.

Father, I repent for these sins on behalf of me and my family to the tenth generation back. I thank You for Your forgiveness and cleansing of these sins. I declare that when I am tested, the Spirit of God will arise within me and bring me into a place of victory. I give You permission in advance of any situation I may encounter that You and Your Holy Spirit may change my actions, words and responses so that I honor You. Please reign and rule over my emotions. Enemy, according to the scripture in James 4:7, as I am now submitted to God, you must flee from me. I command you to take everything that you have put on me, everything that you have tormented me with, every sickness and GO! I command you to pay restitution at no less than a 7-fold return, according to Proverbs 6:31 in every place that you have brought poverty, defeat, robbery, or death and destruction.

Father God, I ask that You cleanse my mind of all unfruitful thoughts, fantasies, and works of the flesh. I thank You for the blood that Jesus Christ has shed on my behalf, and I appropriate the power of His blood and the resurrection power of Your Holy Spirit to every sin, transgression and generational iniquity over myself and my family line. By the power and authority of the blood of Jesus Christ,

I declare my victory. Satan, you no longer have authority to torment me or my children with iniquitous sin patterns. Your plan is cut off now in Jesus name. God has promised in Hebrews 8:12 that He will be merciful to our unrighteousness and our sins and lawless deeds He will remember no more. In Jesus name, amen.

Prayer to Declare the Names of God

Heavenly Father,

I loose myself and my family from demonic attachments that have been invoked for safety, protection, healing, provision, prophecy, and financial blessing. I declare the names of God over every name in heaven, in the earth and under the earth. I declare the name El Shaddai over me and my family, for He is the God that is mighty and He is our sustainer. I declare the name El Elyon over us, for He is exalted as the MOST HIGH GOD. He is exalted as the Sovereign One. I declare Jehovah Nissi over me and my family, for He is the one that causes victory over our enemies. I declare Jehovah Saboath over us, for He is the Lord of Hosts of angelic armies. I declare the name Jehovah Rapha over myself and my household for He is the One that heals. I declare Jehovah Jireh over me and my family, for He is the one that provides. I declare the name of El Gmulot, for He is the God of recompense and the one who spoils the plans of the enemy. I declare the name of Jehovah Mekaddishkem over me and my family for he is our sanctifier. I declare the name of Jehovah Elohim over myself and my household, for it is He who is strong and causes men to fear the Lord. I declare the name of Jehovah Adon over this land, for He is Master, Owner, Lord and my covenant keeping God. I declare the name of Jehovah Roi over us, for the Lord is our Shepherd, protector and keeper. I declare the name of Jehovah Shammah, for the Lord is present. I declare the name of Jehovah Tsidkenu over myself and my family for He is our righteousness. I declare the name of Jehovah Shalom over us, for He is our peace. I release the Spirit of Adoption over myself and my family members, to draw them into personal relationship with the Lord Jesus Christ and to shed abroad the revelation of Abba Father in the hearts of every individual, in Jesus name.

Prayer for Healing from Slander, Gossip and Injustice

Jesus, You are the Son of God, and You are seated victoriously at the right hand of the Father. Today I declare that the enemy is defeated where I am concerned. You are my Master, my Lord and my Savior. Please come with Your Holy Spirit and heal my mind, my emotions, my thoughts, my confession and my memories. I forgive those that failed to reach out to me when I was hurting. I forgive those that have intentionally caused hurt and pain to me and my family, and those that have done it unintentionally. I ask You to bless, heal and deliver those that have acted in ways that have hurt me or caused harm to me or my family. I release the people responsible for my pain to you now.

I will trust You to judge fairly and mete out any justice in these issues. Bless those that have hurt me, lied about me, or deliberately caused harm to me or my family. Please set me free from feelings of rejection, shame and offense. Please heal my trust issues with you and others. Please heal the issues related to my past, my present and my future. Heal my hope, my faith and my love. Heal any areas of grief, heaviness, unbelief, and let the renewed mind of Christ be strengthened and formed in me each and every day.

Thank You for releasing into me a spirit of Faith, a spirit of Obedience, the spirit of Adoption, the spirit of Revelation and Truth. Now tell me Lord, what I need to do as an act of faith that will release my breakthrough. Confirm it and convict me that I will not neglect to do whatever You tell me to do. Thank You for eternal life, health, and victory, and for restoring my life and my future, in Jesus' precious name, Amen.

Prayer for Financial Restoration

Father God,

I thank You that finances are not a big deal for You, but You use financial matters to encourage me to pray according to Your will. You want me to prosper, but You also want my soul to prosper. You want me to pray on behalf of what others need, too. So I come to You and I ask for wisdom. I ask for Your counsel and understanding so that I do not suffer from a lack of knowledge.

I also repent for any wrong attitudes and actions that demonstrate selfishness, worry, fear, complaining or doubt. I repent for failing to have compassion or judging others harshly when they have suffered or struggled financially. I repent of pride. I know that those things do not please you and they do not demonstrate faith. I am grateful, Lord, for my home, my family, and all that you have given to bless my life. I am grateful for You, Lord Jesus. I want You to know that I do value You, and how much You have already done for me. Thank you for being my Savior. Thank you for your love and acceptance and the forgiveness of my sins. I choose to forgive anyone that has offended or hurt me. I release them. I ask You to forgive the sins of my generational line, too. Forgive me and those in my generational line for the sins of idolatry, rebellion, and self will that resisted Your ways. Forgive us if there has been any involvement in the occult and for allowing other influences to govern our ways. I renounce all unholy alliances and ungodly covenants that have been made knowingly or unknowingly.

Father, as a child of God, I submit to You and resist the works of the devil. I resist the spirit of poverty, death and destruction that comes from the evil one. I reject all of his ways. I now take authority over the spirit of Python which constricts. I bind it up in the name of Jesus and I forbid it from restricting my ability to prosper. Give me strategy to overcome the enemy's tactics. I also take authority over poverty and death, and forbid these thieving spirits of death and hell from advancing against me, my family and my livelihood. I tell the enemy, "Be bound, in Jesus name." According to what Jesus has already done on the cross, I command you to be silent, impotent, and void of any and all power. Leave me now, in Jesus name.

I release the Holy Spirit, the Spirit of Truth, to show me any areas of my life that may be hindering me from receiving increase in blessing and prosperity. If I need to be realigned in some way, show me. If there are relational changes that need to take place, show me. Let Your divine connections come forth now, I pray. I speak a release of Prosperity, Promotion, Favor, Blessing and Increase. Forgive me, Lord, for areas of selfishness and greed. I know that I am blessed to be a blessing. Let the work of my hands be blessed. Let fruitfulness and increase be released in my family.

I command all illegal encroachers, both in the natural and spiritual to be removed from that which concerns me and my family. Please let angelic assistance be released to help remove any spiritual hindrances to breakthrough. I declare all curses are broken. Let blessing and favor be released over me, my employment situation, business contacts and finances. I command the enemy to restore everything he has taken, according to Proverbs 6:31, and with a 7-fold increase. I call for inheritances to come forth, both spiritual and natural, and I speak release over myself and entire family. I speak the word of RELEASE over the people in my city. I command all mountains of resistance to be removed, every gate unlocked, and every door that is connected to opportunity to be opened. I speak a release of Your grace, favor, love and restoration to everyone that is in need of Your touch and Your assistance. Thank you, Lord, for moving on behalf of myself and others. In Jesus name, amen.

Prayer to Find the Right Employment

Father God,

I thank You that You are trustworthy. I admit that letting You lead is not always comfortable for me, but I choose to live by faith. I do not want to put limits on what I think You can or will do. Please take me by the hand and lead me into the good plans that You have for me. I need a good paying job that will provide for me and my family. You know my skills and abilities better than anyone. Please help me find the right employment that will also be a joy and a blessing. Your word says the blessing of the Lord adds no sorrow to it. Please give me the blessing of employment that adds no sorrow to it. Father, every time an obstacle appears, I ask You to get me around it. I ask You also to move every mountain out of my path or dig a way through it, but get me connected properly. I ask for You to make divine connections for me and my family, for my friends, and for others in the body of Christ. I pray for the people in my neighborhood and in my city of _____ that they too would have good employment. Holy Spirit, please give me the inspired ideas, creative solutions and the plan of Your design that will help me know what to do next. Let Your thoughts become my thoughts. Those things that are truly of You, let them keep pressing me to take the appropriate action, even if it doesn't make sense in the natural. I choose faith over fear. I thank You for Your sudden interruption in my circumstances to lead me into the blessing you have for me. Tell me what door to knock on, what to ask for, and let Your favor grant my requests. In Jesus name, amen.

Prayer for Healing and Deliverance for Native Americans

Father God, Lord Jesus and Holy Spirit:

I come to You on behalf of myself and all those in my ancestral line that came before me. I ask for Your forgiveness for our sins, and today I acknowledge that many of us sinned by never asking for Jesus Christ to be our Lord and Savior. Many of us committed sins and trespasses in rebellion to Your ways. Please hear my prayer and let the blood of Jesus cleanse my ancestral line from all unrighteousness. I take You as My Lord, and ask that You adopt me as Your child. You paid for me with Your blood, Lord Jesus, and I thank You that You went to the cross in my place.

Father, I also come to you as a citizen of the United States, and I ask You to forgive the sins of our forefathers. I ask You to forgive the sins of those that pioneered and settled this land, and the pagan practices, cultures and traditions brought in from foreign lands. Forgive, I pray, our presidential and political leaders that broke treaties and treacherously removed the boundary lines of Native Americans and others to claim them as their own. For it is written: *"Don't cheat your neighbor by moving the ancient boundary markers set up by previous generations."* Prov. 22:28

Forgive us for encroaching on property that didn't belong to us and cheating rightful heirs out of their inheritance, for it is also written, *"Do not move an ancient boundary stone or encroach on the fields of the fatherless,"* in Proverbs 23:10.

Forgive us for impoverishing Native American families, forcing them out of their homes, for making slaves of other races and nationalities; for causing others to feel overcome with jealousy, fear, anger and desire vengeance against those who treated them wrongfully. Forgive us for the grief we caused, the injustices and the bloodshed. Forgive us for broken covenants, vows and agreements and for the curses that came as a result of those actions. Although I may not have personally taken part in these sins, I understand that there is a need to recognize the sins of those that came before us and I ask for the blood of Jesus to atone for these things so that this land can be cleansed. Please allow all those that have been affected by this generational root of bitterness, grief and poverty now find the grace to forgive, even generations of mistreatment and injustices. I choose to forgive anyone that I have been offended with. I choose to forgive those that I feel are responsible for my pain or bitterness. Please let Your restoration be upon us all. I pray for the blessings that have been blocked up, barricaded, unlawfully stolen, hidden or plundered - and I tell them, "Come back into your rightful generational line! Come back into those families and let the blessings flow abundantly in Jesus name."

Father, I renounce all false gods and masters. According to Your word, O God, in Deuteronomy 7:5, You commanded Your people to destroy ungodly altars and break down their sacred pillars. Let these prayers of renouncement accomplish the destruction of all ungodly altars in my family, in my generational line, and in this nation.

On behalf of myself, my generational line, the founding fathers of this nation and all political leaders in this land, I identify with these sins and the need to acknowledge them to You so that our land may be healed. Therefore, I renounce the demonic spirits of hoodoo, voodoo, Satanism, and all spirits of witchcraft and magic in the name of Jesus Christ. I renounce all practices and demonic spirits associated with black magic. I repent from any traditions or rituals used by the Cherokee, Chickasaw, the Creek, Seminole, Choctaw, the Blackfoot, Cree, Crow, Pauite, Shoebone, Cheyenne, Sioux, the Ute, Pawnee, the Navajo, Shawnee and Apache tribes that had demonic sorcery in the use of their customs and traditions. I renounce African religions, religious works, manmade doctrine and traditions. Forgive me for praying to Catholic saints, patrons and patronesses, invoking familiar spirit guides and any and all other false gods and deities of various religions.

I renounce the use of tobacco for ceremonial or ungodly religious purposes and any and all power associated with it to be rendered impotent, paralyzed and powerless, according to what You have already done on the cross, Lord Jesus.

I renounce all ungodly spirits that may be associated with Native American dances that involve the use of familiar spirits, the use of demonic power, psychic energy, ancient witchcraft practices, sorcery, charms, spells, incantations and magic. Let all ungodly altars be silent and dismantled now. Let the blood of Jesus cover those individuals that have participated in demonic worship whether or not they participated knowingly or unknowingly. I ask You to deliver them and set them free from all deception, Lord Jesus. Let Your Holy Spirit reveal the truth that will free people from demonic oppression. Let the blinders fall off. Give them a spirit of revelation and an understanding heart that they might come to know the One and True Living God, Jesus Christ.

I renounce all customs and dances that involved speaking word curses on their enemies through traditional songs and storytelling. Forgive us for things we did and practices that were accepted that had a spirit of death and cursing bound to the words that were spoken. Let all word curses be broken now in the spiritual and earthly realms. Let those words laced with death lose all power and cease to echo in the spirit realm. I bind the spirit of death that is associated with these customs and culture and forbid the spirits of death and hell from being released. I command them to go back now to the place where Jesus sends them and forever be bound into captivity. I declare that the spirits of death and hell will no longer advance in the name and authority of Jesus Christ.

On behalf of myself, my ancestors and the forefathers of this nation, I renounce demonic attachments associated with gambling and ceremonial gambling. I loose the demonic spirits and spiritual enforcers off of all objects used in gambling and command them to return to the abyss created for all demons. Let the spirits of lust, greed, selfishness and bondage be bound in the name and authority of Jesus Christ. I pray, O God, let the Spirit of Liberty be released to free all people that have been bound by sin and addiction. Let them be loosed from their bondage in Jesus name.

Let all demons be loosed off of individuals, out of homes, offices, businesses, churches, and expelled out of the land that You have given to Your rightful heirs. I ask You, Lord Jesus, to grant an order for eviction from the court of heaven that commands all encroachers, squatters, soothsayers, and those who practice demonic witchcraft off of the land. I command these demonic spirits to be sent back to the place prepared for all demons where they must be bound and confined until the day of their eternal judgment in the lake of fire.

I thank You, Lord Jesus, Heavenly Father and Holy Spirit for releasing Your power against the works of evil, that it might come to a quick and sudden end. I ask that You also release the power of Your Holy Spirit to bring forth forgiveness, compassion, grace and healing. Let there be signs, wonders and miracles, to the glory of the Son of God, Jesus Christ. I ask that You display Your power against the works of darkness, evil and Satan, that the workers of sorcery, demonic magic, witchcraft, spells, incantations, and every form of demonic power would be seen as inferior to that of Your Holy Spirit . I ask that the name of Jesus would be glorified and the enemy be put to an open shame. I ask that everything the enemy has done to conspire, entrap, ensnare, falsely accuse, gain a false judgment by deceit, bribery or falsehood be overturned. Let all who oppress Your children and hinder them from their divine purpose and assignments be stopped and brought to justice. Let righteous judgment prevail. I ask that You would, according to this petition, grant victory and justice for those that have waited for Your intervention. Let the power of Christ be displayed, the name of Jesus glorified, as You destroy the works of the evil one. In Jesus name, amen.

Prayer to Break African Witchcraft

Dear Heavenly Father,

I seek Your help, the help that is only available to me through Jesus Christ, the blood of the lamb, and Your Holy Spirit. I desperately want to be cleansed from demonic spirits, unbroken curses and familiar spirits that have been a part of my life, through my family members, from even before my birth. I ask You, Jesus Christ, Lord of all, to be my Lord and Savior. I ask You to cleanse me from all unrighteousness and set me free.

I repent for any way that I have knowingly or unknowingly given place to demonic spirits and allowed them to access my life. I renounce the sins of my parents, grandparents, and other ancestors and this day I divorce the enemy, Satan, and all other false gods and religions.

I renounce and divorce the enemy, Satan, and any evil spirit that may have been called into my life. I renounce the spirits of Santeria, Lucumi, African gods and all familiar spirits associated with rituals, prayers, customs and traditions. I renounce the seven African spirits known as Papa Legba, Obtala, Oya, Oshun, Chango, Ogun and Yemmaya, in the name of Jesus Christ.

I renounce all Loas, mediums and familiar spirits, ungodly priests, priestesses, sorcerers and wizards.

I renounce fear, self-will, lust, control and confusion. I break every ungodly covenant, oath and vow that may have been spoken by myself or any of my ancestors, knowing that this is forbidden by Your word. Lord Jesus, please let me be released from any ungodly alliances, covenants, or legally binding treaties that were enacted between me, my family, and demonic spirits.

I renounce African and cultural witchcraft, Yoruba traditions, shamans, witch doctors, their rituals and voodoo that have been practiced by my ancestors. I want nothing to do with those practices, rituals, and traditions and I renounce them all, in Jesus name.

I renounce divination and conjuring of all familiar spirits of the dead and those in which my ancestors and family members have participated. I renounce all soul ties to familiar and familial protectors, spirit guides, scribes and messengers, diviners and ungodly priests, false fathers and mothers, and those known as *babalawo*.

I renounce all inanimate objects used for divining purposes, including casting of chains. Lord Jesus, I ask that You break every ungodly chain that has tied me to these things that I am now renouncing.

I renounce all animal and material sacrifices made on my behalf or those in my family line. I renounce all human involvement for the sake of divining information, the use of familiar spirits, spirit guides, and false gods. I renounce all blood that was shed from any source that was tied to my life through the use of occult practices. I renounce all herbalists and root workers that concocted medicines, potions, magic and incantations used in *ayajo*.

I repent and renounce any participation of myself or those in my family line in the indoctrination, apprenticeship, spiritual journey, rituals or rites of passage of myself or others into occult practices.

I renounce all lying, devious, deceptive and manipulative spirits that were inherited as a curse.

I renounce the spirit of fear, suspicion, rejection, loneliness, inferiority, insecurity, poverty, death and hell that have come into my life.

I renounce the spirit of abandonment, unloving spirits, guilt and condemnation.

I renounce all spirits of infirmity.

Father God, Lord Jesus and Holy Spirit, please accept my prayer. I want nothing to do with any of these spirits or their ungodly practices. This day I divorce the enemy and all false gods that have been a part of my life, whether through inherited curses, the sins of my ancestors or my own involvement. Please forgive me and those in my family line. Please wash us clean from this iniquity and let the blood of Jesus cover our sins, and close the doors to the enemy. I ask you to cleanse me from all unrighteousness according to Your word in 1 John 1:9. You said if I confessed my sins, You were able and just to forgive them and cleanse me from this unrighteousness. I submit to Your Lordship, Jesus, and the authority of Your Holy Spirit. I will not serve any other God but You! I ask You to restore my life, my health, my finances, my well being, good, healthy and godly relationships, and bless me the way you want me to be blessed.

Father, I forgive my family members for the hurt they have caused me. I forgive them for releasing curses in my life. I ask You to bless them with revelation and understanding of the error of their ways so that they can find their salvation and deliverance in You, Jesus. Please heal their minds, set their hearts free, and take good care of them. I release them into your hands.

Now, confident that I am forgiven of my own sins, I take the authority that You have given me, and I declare:

In the name and authority of Jesus Christ, I loose myself from all punishing, tormenting and vengeful spirits assigned to my life that would perpetuate a curse.

In the name and authority of Jesus Christ, I declare Him only to be my shield, protector, guardian, and refuge.

I command every demonic chain to be severed from my life in the name of Jesus.

(This next part is included for those seeking future mates or if you are praying for your children's future spouse).

I declare that death and hell no longer have the right to advance against my life, any future children or family members. Father, I pray that you prepare the heart and life of my future spouse (As well as my children's spouses) to also be educated and informed about generational curses. Prepare him/her/them now also, to be cleansed from the iniquity of her bloodlines. Help us/them to be well prepared for one another, and I trust You to bring us together when we are adequately prepared for one another. Let us together raise a family without inherited generational curses, and train our/their children in the ways of the Lord.

I command every demonic spirit on assignment over my life to return to the place that Jesus made for you. Do not come back, I want nothing to do with you and I resist you! According to James 4:7 you must now flee from me, my home and everything that pertains to me. Get out in Jesus name!! Let the curse over my home, myself and my family, and all that pertains to us be broken now, in Jesus name. I thank You, Father, for allowing us to receive Your restoration and the blessings that have been held back. I ask that Your Holy Spirit fill me with love, truth, wisdom, might, a spirit of understanding and enable me to live according to Your commands. In Jesus name, amen.

Prayer for a Resurrection Miracle

Father,

Your word is truth. I believe it, and I'm putting my trust in the integrity of who You are. You are holy. You sacrificed your very own life for me, for my household...and for (*insert name of person for whom you are praying*). Your word says in Romans 8:32, He who did not spare His own Son, but delivered Him over for us all, how will He not also with Him freely give us all things? I believe in You, Lord Jesus. You would not have died in our place if You did not intend to give us what we ask for and need in order to live in health and wholeness. You said in John 10:10 that You came to give us abundant life, so I am asking on (_____'s) behalf, that You give him/her the abundant life that You promised. I stand in faith and remind You of Your promises, and as I declare Your word to You, I ask that You release the power contained in Your word to accomplish all Your will and purpose. I ask You to release angels to carry out the fulfillment of Your promises.

Therefore, in the name and authority that You have given me as Your blood-bought child, and as a co-heir along with Christ, I do declare:

Psalm 68:20

"Our God is a God who saves; from the Sovereign LORD comes escape from death."

Declaration: Father, I thank You that You have saved (_____) and delivered him/her from death according to Your word in Psalm 68:20.

Isaiah 38:16

"O Lord, by these things men live, And in all these is the life of my spirit; O restore me to health and let me live!"
Declaration: Father I thank You that the life of Your Spirit lives in (_____). You have restored his health and let him live according to Isaiah 38:16.

Job 33:25

"Let his flesh become fresher than in youth, Let him return to the days of his youthful vigor; "
Declaration: Father, I thank You that (_____'s) flesh is fresh and youthful, and You have restored his/her vigor according to Job 33:25.

1Kings 19:7-8

"The angel of the LORD came again a second time and touched him and said, "Arise, eat, because the journey is too great for you."
Declaration: Father, I thank You for sending Your angel and Your Holy Spirit to touch (_____) a second, third or even a fourth time, to tell him/her to arise and be healed. Touch

them again as you did for Elijah in 1 Kings 19:7-8, for You are willing to do it.

Psalm 116:8-9

"For You have rescued my soul from death, My eyes from tears, My feet from stumbling."

Declaration: Father, I thank You that You have rescued (_____'s) soul from death according to Psalm 116:8-9.

Ruth 4:14-15

"Then the women said to Naomi, "Blessed is the LORD who has not left you without a redeemer today, and may his name become famous in Israel."

Declaration: Father, I thank You that You have not left (_____) or our family without a redeemer. Redeem his/her life from death so that Your name may become famous once again, according to Ruth 4:14-15.

Titus 3:5-6

"He saved us, not on the basis of deeds which we have done in righteousness, but according to His mercy, by the washing of regeneration and renewing by the Holy Spirit..."

Declaration: Father, I thank You that You have saved (_____) from death not because of his/her own righteousness, but according to Your mercy, by regenerating his/her mortal body and renewing him through Your Holy Spirit, according to Titus 3:5-6.

1 Thessalonians 1:5

"....for our gospel did not come to you in word only, but also in power and in the Holy Spirit and with full conviction; just as you know what kind of men we proved to be among you for your sake."

Declaration: Father, I thank You that the gospel of Jesus Christ is not only in word but in power of Your Holy Spirit. Let the power of Your Holy Spirit now raise (_____) up in complete health and restoration according to Your word in 1 Thessalonians 1:5.

Psalm 30:9

"What is gained if I am silenced, if I go down to the pit? Will the dust praise you? Will it proclaim your faithfulness?"

Declaration: Father, I thank You that You do not benefit from (_____'s) death. Nothing is gained by silencing his voice and robbing him/her from being able to proclaim your goodness. Therefore, according to Your word, let his/her ability to speak and praise You be restored even better than before according to Psalm 30:9.

Jeremiah 17:14

"Heal me, O LORD, and I will be healed; Save me and I will

be saved, For You are my praise."

Declaration: Father, I thank You for healing (_____) and giving him/her the ability to praise you again according to Jeremiah 17:14.

Psalm 41:1

"Blessed is the one who considers the poor! In the day of trouble the LORD delivers him;"

Declaration: Father, I thank You that because (_____) has been kind to the poor and has been a constant source of provision to their family and others, You remember him/her and have delivered him in his day of trouble. Let it be done for him/her now according to Your word in Psalm 41:1.

Jeremiah 39:17

"But I will rescue you on that day, declares the LORD; you will not be given into the hands of those you fear."

Declaration: Father, I thank You that You have rescued (_____) and have not given him/her into the hands of death. We do not fear because you are in control. Deliver (_____) according to Your promise in Jeremiah 39:17.

Numbers 23:19

"God is not human, that he should lie, not a human being, that he should change his mind. Does he speak and then not act? Does he promise and not fulfill?"

Declaration: Father, I thank You that You are so holy and pure that You cannot lie. You don't change your mind on what You've said. You don't make empty promises and then not fulfill them! I EXPECT You to raise up (_____) in health. I EXPECT You to restore his/her life better than before this health crisis occurred, because that's just who you are. You watch over Your word to make sure it comes to pass, so now according to Your word, let it be fulfilled this day for (_____) .

Isaiah 55:11

"So will My word be which goes forth from My mouth; It will not return to Me empty, Without accomplishing what I desire, And without succeeding in the matter for which I sent it."

Declaration: Father, I thank You that Your word is anointed to bear fruit and it will not return to You empty. As I return Your word to You by speaking it out of my mouth, I thank You that it produces life. Let Your word have good success and prosper to accomplish what You have desired it to achieve, in Jesus name, amen.

Declarations to Break the Yoke

In the name and authority of Jesus Christ, I command the yoke on my neck to be broken now, for it is written, that God has brought me out of Egypt and broken the bars of my yoke so that I would no longer be a slave.

- I declare I will no longer wear the yoke of the enemy. I cancel the yokes of false guilt, rejection, regret, debt, poverty, infirmity, hopeless, unbelief, and fear RIGHT NOW in Jesus name!
- I declare a release out of captivity in the name and authority of Jesus Christ!
- I declare prosperity, health and blessing are my portion in Jesus name!
- I declare a release from every man-made, self-imposed yoke and hindrance!
- I declare the Lord Jesus Christ has given me the strength of a wild ox and a fresh anointing to accomplish the very works of God!
- I declare angelic assistance has been release to help me fulfill the work of my hand!
- I declare God has given me a mouth filled with wisdom that the enemy cannot contradict!

In the name and authority of Jesus Christ I declare breakthrough has come to my house this day!

Prayer and Declaration for Business

Almighty God,

I invite You, O God, to be my business partner and show me how to prosper. I invite you, Lord Jesus, into my heart and life to be my Lord and Savior, and I thank You for your forgiveness. I ask Your forgiveness for any wrongdoing committed by myself, business partners, landlords and landowners upon which my business resides. Let me be released from any ungodly oaths or covenants that have been made without Your approval. Let every generational curse be broken now and the blood of Jesus cover those sins. I know that I am in need of godly wisdom, strategy and counsel in order to conduct myself in business in such a way that I can be a blessing to my family and others. I eagerly desire Your blessing and favor upon my home, family and business. Therefore, I declare that I will persevere to conduct my affairs with good character, while upholding honesty, integrity and loyalty to those I serve.

- I declare that mercy and truth are a trademark of my life and employment.
- I declare that I am blessed with creative ideas that are anointed for breakthrough.
- I declare that Holy Spirit has given me strategies for success.

- I declare that I am endowed with inner strength, conviction and courage to avoid temptations that would lead me into the wrong things.

- I declare that I am filled with godly wisdom to know how to implement new ideas.

- I declare that You will guide me to make any changes that are needed, including the best location so that my business will prosper.

- I declare that You will help me correctly identify people's needs and how to offer the products that benefit my customer's needs.

- I declare Holy Spirit counsels me with wisdom that outwits my competitors.

- I declare blessing and favor will overtake me and cause me to inherit the goodness of God.

- I declare that the favor of God supernaturally directs people to do business with me.

- I declare an increase in divine encounters, sales and contracts that increase my business.

- I declare I am blessed to be a blessing to others and Your favor is a testimony of Your goodness in my life. Thank You, Father, for hearing this prayer and declaration and sending forth Your answers. In Jesus name, amen.

Declarations to Break New Ground

In the name and authority of Jesus Christ I declare:
That You, Father, will release a chain of events in this city and this geographic region that will demonstrate the example of the resurrection of the Lord Jesus Christ through signs, wonders, miracles and breakthrough.

- I declare the Holy Spirit is revealing spiritual realities of people's heavenly identities, according to John 16:13.

- I declare the eyes of people in this city and region are opened to discern apostolic and prophetic gifts in God's vessels, and they will heed the word of the Lord.

- I declare a release of spiritual discernment to recognize the difference between ecclesiastical or natural authority vs. genuine spiritual authority.

- I declare people will come out from idolatrous structures and systems and be separated unto God as it is written in 2 Cor. 6:17.

- I declare the queen of heaven is unseated from ungodly thrones, and people have come out of the systems of corruption as it is written in Revelation 18:4.

- I declare the Kingdom of God is confronting demonic structures and systems now, as it is written in Acts 17:30,21 and Acts 19:8.

- I declare people's eyes to be opened and their hearts receptive to receive truth. I declare they are full of hope related to their heavenly calling and purpose, in Jesus name.

- I declare the people in this city and this geographic region will no longer walk according to the evil desires of lust, greed and envy, and they will not fulfill the lusts of the flesh.

- I declare people in this city and this geographic region will lose the desire to pursue selfishness, idolatry and will not be led by unfruitful thoughts and fantasies, in Jesus name.

- I declare the love and mercy of God is released in ever increasing measure in this city and in this region.

- I declare the idolatrous systems in this city and geographic region are overturned as it is written in Judges 6:25-27.

- I declare the ungodly spiritual forces ruling the economic, government, education and religious systems in this city and this region are torn down and the government of the Lord Jesus Christ is established according to Isaiah 9:6.

- I declare a release of persevering faith that breaks open new ground in this city and this region.

- I declare people in this city and this region will experience a great baptism of the Holy Spirit, as it is written in Acts 1:4 and Acts 2:1-4.

- I declare people in this city and region will be born of the Spirit and of the Water through the Holy Spirit and enter the Kingdom of God according to John 3:5.

- I declare people will receive the Holy Spirit by the laying on of hands as it is written in Acts 8:15-18.

- I declare the exponential increase of the power of Holy Spirit to do good works, to heal the sick, to cast out demons, and raise the dead, as it is written in Acts 10:38.

- I declare people in this city and region will have an awakening to the reality that the same spirit that raised Christ from the dead dwells in them, as it is written in Romans 8:11.

- I declare a release of supernatural forgiveness, grace and mercy in Jesus name.

- I declare households and families are coming into right relationship and divine order in Jesus name.

- I declare the passion, authority and fire of God is demonstrated in ever increasing measure.

- I declare an awakening of heart and minds to align with the plans and purposes of the Kingdom of God throughout this city and region, and people will be eager to hear what the Spirit of the Lord is saying to them, as it is written in Acts 10:33.

These things have been declared according to Your promise, Father, in Job 22:28. What we have decided upon shall be established so that light will shine on our ways, in Jesus name.

Strategic Prayer for U.S. Military Troops

Father God,

I pray for Your favor on land, in the airwaves and on sea. I pray for Your favor to help American military troops advance against every enemy, adversary and foe. Empower them to take dominion away from evil men and advance in order to implement justice for the oppressed. Position yourself around them as a shield, and let Your favor grant us everything that is needed to carry out the assignments we have been given.

Give our troops godly wisdom, discernment, the Spirit of Understanding, prophetic insight and foresight. Grant them the ability to formulate and implement excellent strategy against all adversaries and enemies. Help them to be unpredictable to the enemy so that opposing forces cannot predict our military's next move. I ask You to make the enemy's ears deaf to plans being put together by our military. If our enemy's hear about our plans or get tipped off, let them forget all about it like they never heard it. Get our troops behind enemy lines without being seen. I speak blindness into the eyes of our adversaries, opponents and enemies, in Jesus name. Draw their attention elsewhere, Lord. While the enemy is occupied with something else, hit him in his blind spot. Send out the weapons out of your armory that will create fear and confusion in the enemy camp and eliminate his ability to create a strong defense.

Lord Jesus, ride into battle and go before our troops to help them secure the victory. Give those that are on the enemy's side troubling dreams. Show them, like you did to the Midianites in Gideon's day, a dream of American military defeating them. Show them that You are not on their side fighting ungodly battles with them. Show the enemy that You have delivered them into the hands of Your servants and that there is no way they can win. Demoralize the enemy and cause them to lose hope in their ungodly leaders. Let them lose hope in themselves and know that they cannot defeat those that have the King of Kings fighting on their behalf. Turn their hearts and loyalties to come over to the Lord's side, and to act courageous in taking a stand for righteousness. Compel them to do whatever you tell them to do. Let them see themselves surrounded by those they consider their enemies and know they are already conquered.

I ask you to create calculated disorder to weed out, pluck up and remove ungodly authority and all those determined to fight for Satan's agenda. Create enmity where it's needed in order to divide loyalties and tear down the enemy's authority structure. Establish leadership in this nation and in our military that will yield to Your authority and allow Your plans and purposes to be carried out.

I ask You to dispatch angels to lay siege to enemy supply lines and cut off their communication with one another. Squeeze, hinder, interrupt and remove the enemy's ability to gather intel, finances, and supplies. Blow up loyalties between allies and separate enemy forces from one another. Thin out enemy forces and cause them to retreat, give up, and utterly take themselves out of the battle. Feed the enemy's paranoia by convincing them that those they are fighting are superior in every way and have capabilities that they cannot match. Release information that convinces them they have already lost so that they will not attack but allow themselves to be captured. Show American military troops what is on the enemy's horizon and help them develop a plan to unravel enemy schemes.

Rally Your people O Lord, and call for Your angelic army to establish a fortified front against enemy assault. Help Your people, O God, to advance into enemy territory and set up outposts. Enable us to recover what has been lost, taken captive and what the enemy has claimed for himself. Let our prayers come before you and may You send Your help in answered prayer quickly. O Lord, may it bring you great glory. In Jesus name, amen.

Prayer to Enforce God's Dominion in Your City

Abba Father,

I come before you today to give you thanks, to recognize You and You alone as Supreme Authority. I declare Jesus is Lord, over our lives, over our cities, and this nation and specifically over this geographic region.

Lord Jesus, Your words in Mark 3:27 remind us that we must bind the strongman before his house can be divided and his goods taken away. I declare Jesus is King of Kings and Lord of Lords, the MOST HIGH GOD, and I declare Your name above every other name. I command every knee to bow to the name of Jesus Christ our Lord, and I ask You to release your warring angels to bind the strongmen of idolatry, corruption, rebellion and pride in the name and authority of Jesus Christ.

I declare that according to what You have done on the cross and through these prophetic declarations, that these demonic spirits are bound in the name and authority of Jesus Christ. Let Your hand break the power of ungodly altars for in Deut. 12:31 it is written, *"You must not worship the Lord your God the way these other nations worship their gods, they do all kinds of detestable things the Lord hates."* According to the work of the cross of Christ and His resurrection, I command these ungodly spirits to be rendered powerless, impotent, paralyzed and silent.

In the name and authority of Jesus Christ I also bind all mediums and familiar spirits, ungodly priests, priestesses, sorcerers and wizards and any other names which they may be called. I bind any and all inanimate objects from being used in any sort of witchcraft and loose all evil spirits off of individuals, objects, and evil altars. I command them to go to the abyss that was created for them in Jesus name, for it is written in 1 Corinthians 10:14 that we are to flee from idolatry, and again in 1 Cor. 10:20 we are commanded not to be participants with demons.

I release the curse upon all false doctrine and doctrine of devils, and I declare, in the name and authority of Jesus Christ, that the perverse root that brings error must dry up immediately. I declare the perverse root from perverse trees to be cut off from this land and to bear no more fruit, for it is written in Matthew 7:15-20 that bad trees cannot bear good fruit. Let every tree that does not bear good fruit be cut down and thrown into the fire. I declare that evil and perversity will not prosper in Jesus name. Let good trees with their roots in the Lord Jesus Christ be planted in every place where evil trees once prospered.

In the name and authority of Jesus Christ, I ask You to send your warring angels to bind the spirit of Chaos. I release Divine Order and call all things into alignment now, saying, "*Let there be order,*" in Jesus name. I call for unity, healing, restoration, and the glory of the Lord to be released in every home and over this city and region, in Jesus name.

I loose every person from demonic attachments and influences pertaining to false spiritual fathers and mothers. I declare deaf ears are now opened to hear what the Spirit of the Lord is communicating according to Isaiah 35:5 and Isaiah 29:18,19.

I loose every person from demonic attachments and influences pertaining to mind control, emotions, mental illness, depression and insanity. I declare healing, clarity and restoration of sight to those that have been blinded according to Psalm 147:3, Isaiah 42:7 and Isaiah 32:3.

I loose every person from demonic attachments and the curse that brings sickness, disease and infirmity. I declare supernatural healing, restoration and the release of the gifts of Holy Spirit to heal and deliver according to Mark 16:18 and Matthew 11:5.

I loose every person from spirits of poverty, death and hell. I loose honest and reputable businesses from demonic attachments that impoverish, steal and destroy their ability to prosper. I declare the promise in 3 John 1: 2 that as people's souls prosper, they will also enjoy prosperity in every part of their lives, and businesses will prosper. I declare restoration, increase and blessing. I declare raises and promotions, creative and witty ideas, and retroactive compensation to be released. According to Proverbs 6:31 the thief has been caught and he must restore with a 7 fold increase and give up the entire substance of his house. I declare the losses of previous years to be restored to those whose right it is, according to 2 Kings 8:6.

I loose every person from the perverse spirit. I loose individuals from unclean spirits of lust, and all things that are perverse and ungodly. I declare a release of Holy Spirit to bring forth conviction, humility, repentance and a desire for purity in every person in this land. I declare that unholy things will not satisfy and will no longer be sought after. I declare a release of passion and hunger for the Lord to prevail in the hearts and minds of those in this geographic region. I declare that according to Colossians 1:13 people are delivered from the domain of darkness and transferred into the kingdom of God's dear Son, Jesus Christ, and those that hunger shall be filled according to Matthew 5:6.

I loose every person from demonic warring spirits: fear, anger, accusation, jealousy, slander, envy, strife, unforgiveness and bitterness. I release the curse to dry up and cut off the root of war in this land. I declare a release of heavenly wisdom from Holy Spirit; unity, forgiveness and mercy in Jesus name. I declare a release of the light of Christ and the spirit of humility, grace and forgiveness to wash over the hearts and minds of every individual in this land according to 1 John 2:8-10. I declare that people will abide in the light of Jesus Christ and will come into unity now, the unity that releases a great anointing and the glory of God, according to Psalm 133.

I loose every person from demonic attachments that have been invoked for safety, protection, healing, provision, prophecy, and financial blessing. I declare the names of God over every name in heaven, in the earth and under the earth. I declare the name El

Shaddai over this land, for He is the God that is mighty and He is our sustainer. I declare the name El Elyon over this land, for He is exalted as the MOST HIGH GOD. He is exalted as the Sovereign One. I declare Jehovah Nissi over this land, for He is the one that causes victory over our enemies. I declare Jehovah Saboath over this land, for He is the Lord of Hosts of angelic armies. I declare the name Jehovah Rapha over this land for He is the One that heals. I declare Jehovah Jireh over this land, for He is the one that provides. I declare the name of El Gmulot, for He is the God of recompense and the one who spoils the plans of the enemy. I declare the name of Jehovah Mekeddishkem over this land, for he is our sanctifier. I declare the name of Jehovah Elohim over this land, for it is he that is strong and causes men to fear the Lord. I declare the name of Jehovah Adon over this land, for He is Master, Owner, Lord and covenant keeping God. I declare the name of Jehovah Roi over this land, for the Lord is our Shepherd, protector and keeper. I declare the name of Jehovah Shammah, for the Lord is present. I declare the name of Jehovah Tdiskenu over this land for He is our righteousness. I declare the name of Jehovah Shalom over this land, for He is our peace. I release the Spirit of Adoption over every individual and household, to draw people into personal relationship with the Lord Jesus Christ and to shed abroad the revelation of Abba Father in the hearts of every individual, in Jesus name.

I ask now, Father, for angelic assistance to be released to open the heavens and release breakthrough in this land, and in our city. I thank you for hearing my prayer and declarations, and establishing them for all of us so that light will shine on our ways. This you have promised in Job 22:28, and I thank You for watching over your word to perform it. As I have declared these things then I *expect* You to release angelic assistance to enforce my prayers and declarations. I *expect* you to enforce the submission and eviction of the enemy, and I thank You for using my prayer to release Your dominion in my home, this city, and our nation, in Jesus name. Amen.

Conclusion

Every impossible situation is simply there so you can believe. It's there so you can receive something from God that you didn't have before. His gifts are often wrapped in unusual packaging!

Impossible is a lie. Victories are won over impossible situations on a regular basis. Every battle presents an opportunity for a new victory. Every test presents the opportunity for a wonderful testimony. Every miracle must first be presented as an impossible situation. The people who win are the ones that never give up even when all the odds are against them. The greatest victories are often the ones that appear as defeats, and God turns the whole thing around in a surprise comeback.

Don't despise the struggle, for it's the struggle that will lead you to your purpose. Some of history's greatest achievers aren't necessarily famous. God's great achievers are those that wrestle in prayer and refuse to let go until they see the blessing of answered prayer. The wrestling produces the fruit of patience, and it's through faith and patience that we inherit our promises. We must learn to be tenacious with dogged determination that *we mean business,* and we're not leaving our prayer post empty handed.

The things you've overcome are your testimony. When you share your testimonies of what you've overcome, the answered prayer, and your God-given gifts, that is where you will find your purpose. Live with intention to discover where your struggle and your testimonies merge, and you will enjoy great fulfillment. May you live with purpose, joy and expectancy, knowing that we serve a God who shatters impossibilities and invites us to live in a realm where all things become *possible* to those that believe!

Reviews/Comments

"Wow! This is good and long! I think you just about covered everything. I was looking for prayers breaking family strongholds and generational curses and this is a great one thanks!!" - On Breaking Generational Curses, from Missy, Sacramento, CA

"I thought I didn't need this, but since you covered everything, there it was! Thank you, and God bless your ministry." - On Breaking Generational Curses, from Linda S., Florida

"I know it was not of my doing to have found this incredible ministry. I am sure it was my Heavenly Father at work helping me and to see what I would do with it once I found Beyond The Barriers. For He knows the barriers that have hindered me. Reading through the prayers of Beyond The Barriers has been very uplifting, encouraging, and faith building. The prayers have helped me to focus my prayers and be specific, real, and knowing that even when I am praying God already knows. So, I cannot hide or be superficial. My family and I are experiencing some really challenging times as a lot of families. Thanks, James." - On Prayer for Financial Restoration

"Thank you for your story and prayer it really touched my heart...I am praying for a child. I don't have one and never have had one but I know God I working in my favor...I know he will bless me with one in Jesus Name Amen!!!..Thank you again..." - WHITNEY, On Prayer for a Healthy Pregnancy

"Thank you so much for this prayer. I prayed it for my husband, children and myself. Thank you for your ministry. The articles on the spirit of perversion have been so helpful to me! I was molested when I was four and did not realize how the tentacles of this event affected other parts of my life, including beyond the sexual. Thank you again." Anonymous, On Prayer to Be Healed From Sexual Sins

"I added three of your healing prayers to my website today. Many blessings and more be multiplied!" - Gretchen McDevott

"I continue to be led to SHARE your anointed prayers. They are so awesome my sister, as is your humble spirit, and the wisdom the Lord has given you to share! May He continue to bless and provide for you and your husband, your ministry, and may He bless your seed and surround them with angels and favor." - T.F., Indianapolis, Indiana

"...I stopped with my jaw open because yesterday morning I felt the presence of the Holy Spirit come upon me right before I was ready to leave for work. I found myself seeing and stating things I am divorcing myself from. When I saw what you wrote about divorcing the enemy I got the biggest confirmation....Thank you...I thank God for answering my prayer and leading me to you blog...Truly a blessing. Love and much blessings to you and your family." - K.B.

"I am just so happy to have found your writings and blog. THANK YOU for sharing so many helpful and life changing inspirations! God bless!" Amber H.

Manufactured by Amazon.ca
Bolton, ON